Context, Context, Context

How Our Blindness to Context Cripples Even the Smartest Organizations

Barry Oshry

Published in this first edition in 2018 by:
Triarchy Press
Axminster, England

info@triarchypress.net
www.triarchypress.net

A catalogue record for this book is available from the British Library.

Print ISBN: 978-1-911193-28-9
ePub ISBN: 978-1-911193-29-6

Although we are by all odds the most social of all social animals – more interdependent, more attached to each other, more inseparable in our behavior than bees – we do not often feel our conjoined intelligence.

Lewis Thomas,
The Lives of a Cell

Contents

Context, context, context

This is the story of a single organization – Dynamics Unlimited – and its struggle to achieve excellence.

There are millions of organizations in the world; Dynamics Unlimited is one. Nothing special about it. Yet I promise you: its story will shed light on the stories of *all* organizations – yours and others, from the tiniest to the super-sized, from the local to the globalized, non-profit and for-profit, educational and government, church and the military. All of them will find themselves in the story of Dynamics Unlimited.

Its tale will take you deep into the consequences of context-blindness, how it permeates system life, how it corrodes potentially creative and supportive relationships, how it constricts human spirit, and squashes the contributions of human systems.

Going from context-blindness to context-sight is like turning the light on in a darkened room. Now we see choice where before there was no choice. And the choices we see in the light are far from minor adjustments; they confront us with the potential for transforming who we are and who we will become in all the systems of our lives; and they have the potential for fundamentally transforming all the human systems of which we are a part.

So, come along with me as we witness Dynamics Unlimited's journey from context-blindness, with all its costs, to context-sight and the world of transformative possibilities that it reveals. Because DU's journey is also your journey and mine.

A note about Top, Middle, Bottom, and Customer

In this work as well as in others, I regularly refer to Top, Middle, Bottom, and Customer. Sometimes, I inadvertently give the impression of these being *people*, as if there are Tops, Middles, Bottoms, and Customers roaming the world. There are no such people. Top, Middle, Bottom, and Customers are familiar contexts in *all* systems, whether of the flattened participatory type or the multi-leveled hierarchical ones. Most of us in organizational life know what it is like to move in and out of these contexts. It is true that some of us spend more time in one context than the others, thus we become identified with that context. So, for example, we become Tops, even though we know that in other interactions – dealing with the Board or government regulators for example – we are often in Bottom contexts; and in still others we are in Middle or Customer contexts. So, although these terms are applicable to hierarchy, as they are in the tale that follows, they are by no means limited to hierarchy.

The Scene

A conference Room at MICROSCOPE, Inc. A meeting between a recently hired team member (HE) and MICROSCOPE's Chief Contextual Thinker (SHE)

SHE: Congratulations on joining MICROSCOPE.

HE: Really, that's all it took. This was the fastest selection process I've ever been through.

SHE: We know talent when we see it.

HE: See it. See what? I didn't do anything.

SHE: Before the interview. While you were waiting.

HE: I was reading the paper. Doing the crossword puzzle.

SHE: That's what clinched it.

HE: Reading the paper?

SHE: The crossword puzzle.

         It says a lot about what we're looking for. A desire to solve. Looking for the variety of possible meanings in clues. Seeing patterns. Being able to shift one's viewpoint. Finding wholes that make sense of the parts. That covers much of our basic skill set.

HE: And how does this considerable talent of mine fit in with MICROSCOPE's work?

SHE: Let's take a case. An assignment we've been working on lately: Dynamics Unlimited.

HE: I'm ready to dig in.

SHE: First, some background on the company.

Chapter 1: THE PLAN

SHE: Dynamics Unlimited had been a successful company since its founding 15+ years ago. In the last couple of years, however, the company has experienced a severe downturn resulting from a variety of events and conditions: disruptive competition, new technology, changing workforce demographics, globalization, and unpredictable patterns of governmental regulations.

HE: A familiar story.

SHE: Yes, and a recent organizational survey revealed what everyone already knew: low employee engagement, distrust of management, insecurity, rapid employee turnover, low morale, and widespread customer dissatisfaction.

HE: And your assignment was to turn this ship around?

SHE: Actually, no, not at first anyway.

HE: Please explain.

SHE: Well, the Tops had an emergency meeting.

HE: With everyone?

SHE: No, just Tops. *Enough is enough. We need to restore our excellence.* That was the message.

HE: And the next question was *How*?

Enter THE PLAN

SHE: The Tops interviewed several consulting firms. One offered what the Tops felt was an intriguing possibility – called THE PLAN. They assured the Tops that THE PLAN was the key to achieving DU's goal: Renewed Excellence! DU was in dismal shape; THE PLAN promised hope, so a desperate Top team gave it a try.

HE: I've never heard of THE PLAN.

SHE: Allow me to describe it.

THE PLAN for total system empowerment

SHE: According to THE PLAN, all organizations, in fact all human systems, are organic entities engaging with ever-changing environments. In these environments, there are dangers to be avoided and opportunities to be taken advantage of. The fundamental business of all such systems is to survive in their environments and, if possible, thrive by successfully coping with dangers and prospecting among opportunities.

A system in an environment of dangers and opportunities

HE: Surviving and thriving. Coping and prospecting. Sounds like lyrics for a country song.

SHE: With too many unhappy outcomes.

HE: Tell me more.

SHE: THE PLAN is based on the idea that each part of a system – Top, Middle, Bottom, and Customer – because of its position, has a unique contribution it *can* make to the system's ability to survive and thrive.

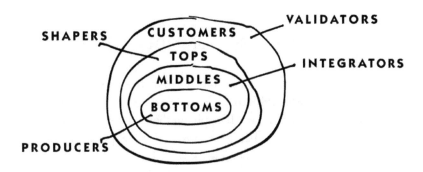

Shapers, Producers, Integrators, Validators

SHE: According to THE PLAN, the system needs Tops to function as SYSTEM SHAPERS, Workers as SYSTEM PRODUCERS, Middles as SYSTEM INTEGRATORS, and Customers as SYSTEM VALIDATORS.

When all this is happening, excellence is sure to follow.

HE: *When* all of this is happening.

SHE: That *is* the point.

Tops as System SHAPERS

SHE: According to THE PLAN, Tops are uniquely positioned to function as the SHAPERS of the system. They do this by looking *outward*, scanning DU's environment: What are the dangers out there, present and emerging? And what are the possibilities, the opportunities, to be taken advantage of? And the Tops shape the system by looking *inward*, seeing that the system has the structure, processes, and resources for coping with the dangers and prospecting among possible opportunities.

HE: So, as I understand it, this isn't necessarily what Tops do; it's what they *can* do.

SHE: Exactly. Given their unique position, this is the contribution Tops *can* make to DU's ability to survive and thrive: Be the system's SHAPERS.

HE: A reasonable goal.

SHE: We'll see.

Workers as System PRODUCERS

SHE: Workers are uniquely positioned to function as system PRODUCERS. As PRODUCERS, Workers are the expert resources regarding work, applying their creative energies to the work of the system, being responsible for the quality of work, finding ways of improving work, working closely with DU's customers. This is the unique contribution Workers can make to DU's ability to survive and thrive.

HE: So this is more than simply showing up for work and doing your job.

SHE: Exactly. This is about being the expert responsible force for how work is done in the organization.

Middle as the System's INTEGRATING MECHANISM

HE: And what does THE PLAN have in mind for the Middles?

SHE: Middles are uniquely positioned to function as the integrating mechanism of the organization, like the integrating mechanisms of the human body: nervous, vascular, and hormonal systems that coordinate, balance, and integrate whole-body processes.

HE: Aren't they supposed to lead or manage?

SHE: They do that. They manage, supervise, coach, mentor. That's what they do *individually*. But their *collective* function, according to THE PLAN, is to integrate the system.

HE: And how do they do this?

SHE: They integrate the system by integrating with one another, sharing information, coordinating system parts, seeing that Tops, Workers, and Customers receive the information and resources they need, seeing that the parts feed and support one another in service of the whole. That's how they function as the system's INTEGRATING MECHANISM.

HE: OK. I see the connection to the body's integrating mechanisms.

SHE: That's the idea. THE PLAN is all about treating the organization as a highly functioning organic system.

HE: OK, so how do the Customers fit?

SHE: Well, if you think of the organization as a human body, then, in a way, the Customers are the organization's personal physicians. The doctors who tell you the truth.

Customers as System VALIDATORS

SHE: According to THE PLAN, customers are uniquely positioned to function as VALIDATORS of the system, letting DU know how well it is doing what it is supposed to be doing. Is it living up to its potential?

HE: Like a reality check.

SHE: Exactly. They validate the system by giving it feedback – positive and negative. Like good doctors, they not only evaluate, they recommend: what to stop doing, needed actions to take. And even if Customers were to sever their relationship with the organization, their feedback and recommendations as VALIDATORS would be informative. That's their unique contribution.

Power is everywhere

HE: So, as I see it, in THE PLAN, all parts of the organization have their unique power to contribute to the overall power of the system.

SHE: Exactly. Power is distributed throughout rather than located at the Top. Each part understands the critical and unique role it plays in ensuring system survival and development. As each part embraces *its* power, the power of the whole flourishes.

HE: What I'm also seeing is how these functions all work together.

SHE: That's also the point. The better Tops are as Shapers, the better conditions will exist for Workers to Produce. The better Middles are at Integrating, the more supported Tops and Workers are in Shaping and Producing. And the better Customers are at

Validating, the more the organization as a whole knows how well it is doing what it needs to be doing.

HE: What a plan!

SHE: You seem enthused.

HE: It's lovely, very simple, elegant. It's got a lot going for it. Top to Bottom, everyone feels their unique value, how the system depends on *them*. It's not the usual perspective, where all power and wisdom lies at the Top. I like that.

SHE: Anything else?

HE: I also like the fact that each part supports the others, *and* that each *depends* on the others. If Tops don't shape, it all falls apart; the system doesn't have the structure it needs for coping and prospecting. If Workers don't produce, it doesn't work. If Middles don't integrate, there's no coordination. And if Customers don't validate, the system just goes on living in fantasy land.

SHE: Very neat. The parts supporting one another *and* depending on one another. What could go wrong?

HE: I'm guessing: plenty.

SHE: Right again. THE PLAN is good; it just wasn't working.

The Summary Report: Part A

❖ *Tops too burdened to function as SHAPERS.*

❖ *Workers too oppressed to function as PRODUCERS.*

❖ *Middle too torn to function as the INTEGRATING MECHANISM.*

❖ *Customers too righteously screwed to function as VALIDATORS.*

SHE: Surveys were conducted, interviews held, results tabulated, and the picture that emerged was disheartening to say the least. Here are some highlights from the interviews.

Feedback from the Tops

"We're too busy to Shape; there are just too many day-to-day issues for us to deal with. Unanticipated changes. Tough decisions to make. We're mostly agreed that Shaping is important but it just isn't possible under present circumstances. Maybe when things lighten up."

Feedback from the Workers

"We're not getting the support we need to produce. Our Middles are weak, uninformed; they don't have the information or resources we need to do our work. And Tops? They're invisible. We're suspicious about what's really behind THE PLAN. Is this just another management trick: more work, less money? Who knows?"

Feedback from the Middles

"Integrating with other Middles never happened. We've all been too tied up in our own business, trying to please Tops and Workers and not being very successful with either. Life in the Middle is simply too exhausting to tolerate more meetings."

Feedback from the Customers

"Dynamics Unlimited is hardly dynamic... I'm treated more like a problem than an opportunity... We're on the lookout for alternative suppliers... Delivery delays... Quality unsatisfactory... Excuses, excuses... We are the customers after all. We're entitled!"

HE: So, what happened next?

SHE: The Tops decided to drop THE PLAN. It seemed to be causing more problems than it was solving.

HE: And the consultants?

SHE: The Tops decided to drop them too. Same reason. Then they interviewed a few other consultants; and finally they settled on us.

HE: What drew them to you?

SHE: After they went into all the details of their unhappy experience with THE PLAN, how it didn't work for *anyone*, they asked us what *we* would do.

HE: And you said?

SHE: Implement THE PLAN.

HE: THE PLAN? You were kidding.

SHE: Not at all. THE PLAN was never the problem. The problem lay in ignoring the *contexts* into which THE PLAN was introduced.

HE: Contexts?

SHE: Contexts. *Putting it all in context.* That's more than a motto; it's the essence of MICROSCOPE's work.

HE: I'd love to understand the "essence of your Work."

Chapter 2: The Essence of MICROSCOPE

SHE: Our work at MICROSCOPE is to help people *see their systems* more clearly. Make the invisible visible. See the contexts in which we live and work. And this is the big part: *to see how those contexts shape our experiences of ourselves, others, our systems, and other systems.*

HE: Can you say a bit more about context?

SHE: Context is the world we are living in... *before* we are living in it. It's the world we are about to enter... *before* we enter it.

It's the temperature and turbulence of the ocean waters *before* we jump in. The heat of the flame before we touch it.

It's the different set of conditions we find in the different places we go.

It's as if physicists were describing the forces operating in the space we are about to enter.

It's the set of conditions whoever enters that context will experience.

There is us, the space we are about to enter, and then there's the experience we have once we enter. It's People in Context and the Experience they are having.

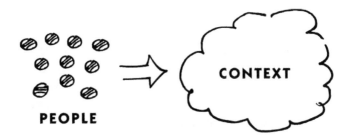

There's Us and the Context we are in

HE: Context, conditions, world, environment, space.

SHE: As you'll see, we tend to use the terms interchangeably.

The point is this: When we are blind to context – which we often are – we are at its mercy. *It does it to us.* We react reflexively to context in ways that cause us debilitating stress, weaken or destroy our relationships, diminish our effectiveness and the quality of our contributions.

HE: All because we're blind to context?

SHE: That's a big piece of it.

HE: And the work of MICROSCOPE?

SHE: Seeing and choosing. Awareness and choice. Awareness is step one. Making the invisible visible. Helping people become aware of the contexts they and others are living in; helping them see how context is shaping their experience. In this case, how context is shaping Dynamics Unlimited's receptivity to THE PLAN.

HE: And step two?

SHE: Instead of being victimized by context, helping people learn how to master the contexts they are in.

HE: So this was your approach: Putting THE PLAN in context?

SHE: Exactly. That is always our approach. *Putting it all in context.*

Generally, we do not see contexts. All we see are people interacting with one another.

Some interactions are going well, some not so well. We have our reactions to one another, our judgments, evaluations, and our explanations of why things are going the way they are going.

But when we lift the veil on these interactions and see what lies beneath, a very different picture emerges.

HE: Lifting the veil?

SHE: A figure of speech. Lift the veil. Make the invisible visible. The point is: We see that Tops, Middles, Workers, and Customers are not simply people meeting people; they are engaging with distinctly different contexts, and each context creates its own challenge to implementing THE PLAN.

HE: Start with me. Help me see these contexts.

SHE: We'll get into these in some detail, but, in a nutshell:

DU's Tops are living in a world of complexity, accountability, and uncertainty. These are the conditions they are contending with.

The Workers are living a world of vulnerability, coping with decisions and actions coming at them from above, decisions and actions that are affecting their lives in major and minor ways.

Middles are living in a tearing world, attempting to cope with the conflicting needs, demands, and priorities coming at them from the Tops, from the Workers, the Customers, and from one another.

And Customers are living in a world of neglect in which products and services are not coming to them as fast as they want, at the quality they feel they deserve, and at a price they consider reasonable.

HE: Hold on a minute! Aren't all parts of the system experiencing *all* of this? Everyone's world is complex; everyone's feeling vulnerable; everyone feels neglect; I suppose everyone's torn between one thing or another. Am I right?

SHE: You are right, of course. So, what we are looking at here is this: What is the *predominant* set of forces operating in each world? What stands out? What *particularly* characterizes each world and differentiates it from others?

HE: OK, I'll go with that. So what's next?

SHE: We're about to see how THE PLAN was experienced in each of these worlds.

Part I

People in Context

Chapter 3: How THE PLAN showed up in the Top Context

The Top World is a world of complexity/accountability/uncertainty

SHE: DU's Tops, like most Tops, particularly in turbulent times, are living in an environment of complexity, accountability, and uncertainty. Lots of inputs to deal with. Complex issues, issues that Tops thought were taken care of elsewhere in the organization, keep coming back. Emerging disruptive technologies. Globalization. New employee demographics. New competitors. Changing regulations. Questions for which there are no clear-cut answers: Grow fast or slowly? Risk or caution? Stick to what we know or move in new directions? Create a collaborative environment with our employees or maintain clear role and power distinctions? These are just some of the issues DU's Tops were dealing with.

HE: That's a fairly familiar Top story.

SHE: Yes it is. So now, put yourself in that Top context. This is all the stuff you are dealing with, worrying about, waking up in the middle of the night thinking about.

HE: And here comes THE PLAN.

SHE: Here comes THE PLAN. This golden opportunity to transform your organization. How does THE PLAN show up in your context?

HE: When they were first presented with it, it probably sounded like an idea with promise. The road to excellence.

SHE: And now?

HE: Hmm. And now they just don't have the energy for it.

SHE: So there it is. Into this world of complexity comes THE PLAN. DU's Tops do see value in the PLAN, but given their current context, they experience it as another complication, and a big one. *Maybe when things calm down, we'll give it a second look.*

HE: So, in this Top World, the Marvelous PLAN, this road map to the future, shows up as one more complication in an already complicated world.

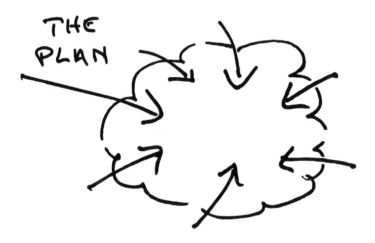

The plan showing up as just another complication

SHE   Exactly. And so long as Tops cannot manage the complications in their world, SHAPING will continue to be out of reach.

Top Complexity is compounded by the Dance of Blind Reflex

SHE: The Tops' situation is further complicated by the power of the Dance of Blind Reflex with its endless opportunities for Tops to reflexively suck responsibility up to themselves and away from others, which only adds to their burden.

HE: Whoa! Slow this down for me. What is this Dance of Blind Reflex?

SHE: Not only are we blind to the context we are in, we are also blind to our *reactions* to context.

HE: I need an example.

SHE: Sure. In the face of all this complexity, there is something we do as Tops – not always, not everyone, but with great regularity. It becomes crystal clear to us that *we are responsible* for handling it all. It's not like a conscious choice we make; it simply happens, like a reflex. It's clear: *We are responsible.*

HE: That can't help things.

SHE: Right. It can only make things worse.

HE: So, not only is their world complex, they add to the complexity by sucking responsibility up to themselves and away from others.

SHE: The more complex their world, the more they suck it up, which increases complexity, and on and on it goes.

HE: A vicious cycle.

SHE: It surely is.

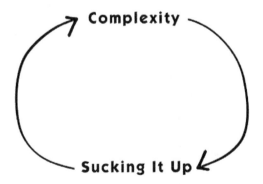

Sucking up responsibility is a poor strategy for reducing complexity

HE: I'm beginning to see the implications for THE PLAN.

SHE: In THE PLAN, Tops function as system SHAPERS. This requires them to see the whole, to be aware of the dangers and opportunities in DU's environment. To look inward, to ensure that DU has the structure, resources, and culture to cope with dangers and prospect among opportunities.

HE: So long as Tops become mired in sucking up endless responsibility to themselves and away from others, SHAPING is not a possibility.

SHE: Exactly.

HE: Time for some awareness.

SHE: Exactly. So our work with Tops is to help them become aware of the part they play in increasing their own burden and the consequences this is having for them, others, and their role as system SHAPERS.

HE: Tops, stop sucking up responsibility!

Caution!

SHE: However, proceed with caution. Never tell Tops that they are burdened *because* they suck up responsibility. That could be the end of your relationship. They will feel, with good reason, that you simply do not understand their world. They *are* burdened by all they are dealing with, that's the reality. What they're not seeing is how their reflex response is adding to that burden. So, be warned.

HE: Got it. I have been forewarned.

SHE: Tops desperately want to succeed, so we need to help them see how what they are doing reflexively works against their success.

HE: Clever. They need to see how they are sabotaging their own interests.

SHE: Exactly. Not only are they burdening themselves, making it more difficult to do the work they feel they need to do, but they are also infantilizing others, depriving them of needed opportunities to test themselves, learn, grow, and bring their own brain power to bear on issues that Tops alone are facing.

HE: It's paradoxical.

SHE: In what way?

HE: They're facing all these complex issues and at the same time limiting the brainpower available for dealing with them.

SHE: That's precisely what *they* need to see.

HE: MICROSCOPE to the rescue.

SHE: Not so simple. There is still the challenge Tops are facing, dealing with the complexity, uncertainty, and accountability in their world.

HE: And the answer is?

SHE: Not so much an answer as a challenge. What if Tops saw the complexity that's causing them such difficulty as an opportunity?

HE: Complexity as opportunity. That would be quite a twist.

SHE: Think about it. Complexity is an opportunity to strengthen *others* in the system. Involve others in these issues. Delegate. Mentor. Coach. *Develop others to do what now only you can do.* Use complexity to strengthen the whole system.

HE: A challenging thought. How are the Tops responding to it?

SHE: They're wrestling with it. For some it's a huge shift.

HE: I can imagine.

She: There are challenges. Loss of control is a real issue. *What if the others don't handle their new responsibilities competently? In the end, I am still accountable.*

HE: There is risk. I can see that.

SHE: And there are issues, real or imagined, around ego. *Am I Top because I have more brain power than the others?*

HE: How do you handle that?

SHE: As you said. It's a risk. It has to be tested. And we always need to remind them of the alternative.

HE: The Dance of Blind Reflex.

SHE: With all its costs.

HE: So now what do you do?

SHE: At this point, *we* don't do anything. Awareness is our business, choice is theirs. We hold up an alternative, and then it's up to them.

HE: And the alternative you hold up?

SHE: The Top Empowerment Stand.

HE: Stand?

SHE: A stand. If you don't want to be one of these blind, reflexive, suck it up, over-burdened Tops, what is your stand for the kind of Top you choose to be?

So, on each Top's desk, there is this card:

My Top Empowerment Stand

*In the presence of complexity, uncertainty, and
accountability,
conditions that will not go away,
instead of sucking responsibility up to myself
and away from others
and becoming the Burdened Top,
My stand is to be a Top who creates responsibility in others.
My stand is to create a system in which responsibility is
experienced throughout.*

HE: And how's this working?

SHE: It's a work in progress.

*

HE: Let me see if I understand MICROSCOPE's approach.

SHE: We call it People-in-Context.

HE: People-in-Context. Good. So, first, you clarify the context people in any part of the system are living in.

SHE: Correct.

HE: Then you help them see how this new initiative – THE PLAN in this case – is experienced in that particular context.

SHE: Correct. Noticing what the context is doing *to* you.

HE: And we usually don't see that.

SHE: Not usually.

HE: And, in our blindness to the context, rather than make things better, we make them worse.

SHE: The Dance of Blind Reflex.

HE: And then, the goal is to help them see a better way.

SHE: Better *and* challenging.

HE: OK. I think I see it.

SHE: Fine. So now let's see how People-in-Context is playing out with Dynamics Unlimited's Workers.

Chapter 4: How THE PLAN showed up in the Bottom Context

SHE: Recently the job titles for DU's Workers were changed from Employees to Associates, but, beyond that, nothing much has changed.

HE: Team One. Associates. Partners. I've been there. Call them what you want, in their hearts they know who they are. They're Workers – on the Bottom.

SHE: They're still living in this world of vulnerability and disregard; on the receiving end of decisions and actions influencing their lives in major and minor ways. THEY – Middles and Tops – are always doing something *to* them.

The Bottom World is a world of vulnerability and problem disregard

SHE: Changes come at them over which they have little or no say. THE PLAN is just one more item coming at them from above: reorganizations, changing skill requirements, retraining. And DU's Workers are living in an environment with lots of untended problems: things that are wrong in their situation – insufficient resources, no feedback on their actions, little recognition, conflicting messages from above. Plus, they see things that are wrong with DU's overall operation – fixes that don't fix anything, directions that make no sense, lack of coordination among Worker groups, unfair treatment. And Workers feel it's Tops' and Middles' responsibility to fix these problems, and they are not fixing them; their issues are disregarded.

HE: So, into this context, comes THE PLAN.

SHE: Again, put yourself in that Bottom context.

HE: It's not a totally unfamiliar spot for me.

SHE: So how are you experiencing THE PLAN?

HE: I'm hesitant. Wondering what's behind this? On paper it sounds interesting, reasonable. *This PRODUCING business might make our work lives more interesting. Using our brains. Working closely with Customers. Being the experts on work. That's got a nice ring to it.*

SHE: I hear a "but" coming.

HE: But… I'm suspicious. There have been similar PLANS in the past. Nothing came of them. *Maybe we should just wait, and this too shall pass. Is this some new management trick, another more work/less money PLAN?*

SHE: And Workers heard rumors about DU shipping some or all of their operation overseas. We are not feeling very secure here.

HE: So, instead of PRODUCING looking like a golden opportunity, in this Bottom context it shows up as more vulnerability.

SHE: And one more set of problems no one's taking care of.

HE: So much for well-intentioned plans.

The Plan showing up as more vulnerability

The Bottom Dance of Blind Reflex

SHE: Exactly, and on top of this comes the Dance of Blind Reflex.

HE: So, once again, we are not only blind to the context, we are also blind to our reactions to it. Is that it?

SHE: You are getting the hang of things.

HE: The Dance of Blind Reflex.

SHE: In this environment of untended problems it's easy for DU's Workers to fall into the Top/Bottom Dance of Blind Reflex, where they, as Workers, reflexively hold higher-ups responsible for their condition and for the condition of the system. They say *"It's their responsibility, not ours, to fix these problems."*

The Top/Bottom responsibility dance

HE: This goes nicely with the Top part of the dance.

SHE: What are you seeing?

HE: Tops suck up responsibility to themselves, and Workers hold higher-ups responsible.

SHE: Exactly. That's what makes it such a neat dance. Everyone's in agreement. Tops are responsible, Workers not responsible. And once again, this is not a conscious choice that Workers make; it simply happens. It becomes crystal clear to DU's Workers that higher-ups are responsible for fixing the problems they are experiencing.

SHE: So again, put yourself in that Bottom World. There are all these problems, things that are wrong with your situation, things that you see are wrong in the organization. You're experiencing these problems, yet you are not feeling any personal responsibility for them. It is crystal clear to you that you're not responsible for these problems, *they are.*

HE: I've been there.

SHE: So what were you feeling?

HE: It's all about *them.* I'm angry at *them.* Disappointed with *them.* Seeing *them* as insensitive, incompetent, maybe even malicious.

SHE: And notice just how much blaming THEM is helping with all these problems you are experiencing.

HE: (Ponders.) Not much. Maybe not at all.

SHE: It's worse than that. Holding higher-ups responsible simply makes things worse. *See, they're* still *not fixing these problems.*

HE: So, holding THEM responsible *increases* the Bottom experience of disregard and all the feelings that go with it.

SHE: And so the cycle goes on and on. Holding others responsible increases the feeling of being disregarded. For which we hold others responsible, and on it goes.

Holding higher-ups responsible is a poor strategy for fixing problems

HE: This is not looking good for THE PLAN.

SHE: Not good at all. In THE PLAN, Workers should function as system PRODUCERS – in charge of work, experts on work, focused on improving work processes, and increasing customer satisfaction. Totally committed to the organization's success. As of now, DU's Workers are a long way from that possibility. So long as they continue to see higher-ups as responsible for fixing problems and improving conditions, PRODUCING will not be a possibility.

HE: That's clear.

SHE: So our work is help Workers become aware of the part they are playing in their own oppression, and the consequences this is having for them, others, and Dynamics Unlimited.

HE: This could look like blaming the victim.

Caution!

SHE: It could. And you would reinforce that image by implying that Workers are feeling oppressed *because* they're holding higher-ups responsible. They will dismiss you as being completely out of touch with the reality of their situation. Tops and Middles *are* causing them problems by their actions and inactions. That's the reality. What Workers are not seeing is how their reflex responses are adding to that oppressed experience and perpetuating that experience.

HE: I still see this as a difficult situation to change.

SHE: And it can be. There are few things more compelling and more difficult for all of us to let go of than experiencing ourselves as the righteous victims of others. It can be a deeply satisfying experience.

HE: And it doesn't require anything from *us*. It's up to others to fix things. We can just sit, suffer, and fume.

SHE: So that's our challenge. It's clear what's gained by being this oppressed Worker. (We can say it's not our fault.) But we have had to work with Workers to see what is lost.

HE: Quite a bit.

SHE: Really! What losses do you see?

HE: The problems may never get fixed.

SHE: That's clear.

HE: Your health could suffer. Anger. Stress. Blood pressure. Heart attacks. Anger wears on you.

SHE: It does.

HE: Work is boring.

SHE: Without recognizing your part in *making it boring*.

HE: You're using the smallest part of your potential.

SHE: Such a waste.

HE: Your relationship with Middles and Tops is that of a whiny child to the grown-ups.

      You get little satisfaction from the work you do.

      You have none of the fulfillment that comes with contributing.

SHE: You seem to be an expert at this.

HE: Like I said, I've been there. You don't have to be a Worker to make yourself Bottom.

SHE: Well said. And offsetting all of that is the satisfaction of being a righteous victim.

HE: That's the challenge.

SHE: This becomes our work.

      First, acknowledge the reality of the condition of Vulnerability and the Disregard that Workers are experiencing.

      Then, help them see how their reflexive response – holding higher-ups responsible – may make them feel self-righteous, but it's not an effective strategy for dealing with the problems they face. And to see clearly the negative consequences this is having for themselves, their relationships, and the system.

HE: And the *opportunity* here?

SHE: To explore with them the possibilities of living fuller, more satisfying lives in the organization, having more agency in their lives, using more of their human potential, contributing.

      The work is to help Workers explore how organizational life would be much more interesting, challenging, and enlivening if, instead of holding others responsible for their condition and the condition of DU, they saw themselves as active, responsible players in making those problems, and other problems that arise, disappear.

HE: I still see resistance.

SHE: You'd do better to think of resistance as *transitional turbulence*.

HE: Which means it could go either way – continue to resist or explore a new possibility.

SHE: Exactly. Keep in mind: Awareness is *our* business, choice is *theirs*. We clarify the current condition and hold up an alternative. Then it's up to them.

HE: And the alternative you're suggesting?

SHE: The Bottom Empowerment Stand.

HE: Taking a stand for the kind of Worker you choose to be.

SHE: Exactly.

The Worker Empowerment Stand
In the presence of Worker Disregard,
a condition that will not go away,
instead of holding higher-ups responsible for my condition
and the condition of the system,
and becoming the Oppressed Worker,
my stand is to be a Worker who is responsible for my
condition in the system and for the condition of the system.

HE: This is a huge shift you're asking Workers to make.

SHE: Some jump to it. Others are hesitant. And others are firmly shut down. We're asking them to explore the possibility. Try it out. See what changes it can produce in their lives. In the end it's *their* choice.

HE: I'm feeling my own resistance… um, transitional turbulence. *Shouldn't higher-ups be fixing these things? Why us?*

SHE: You would think so, wouldn't you? But try looking at this another way. What if Workers saw problems as opportunities? What if *you* did?

HE: Opportunities! You're kidding.

SHE: Not really. Problems are challenges, opportunities to test oneself, explore one's potential, grow. Be in charge of your life. Problems are good! At least, they can be. Consider life without problems to solve.

HE: Like life in a nursing home, where there are no problems for you to solve. All your needs are handled.

SHE: And then you die.

HE: I take your point, but I still see this as a hard sell.

SHE: It is. It's a transformative shift for all of us as Workers. No minor adjustment. There are personal challenges – for you, for them, for all of us. *Do I really want to give up blaming others? It is so satisfying. Do I really want to give up my passivity? It is so relaxing not to have to take any action. Do I really want to give up my sense of injustice; after all that's why THEY (Tops) get the big bucks.* All of that. And, these are the issues DU's Workers need to deal with if they choose to function as system PRODUCERS and experience the personal satisfaction that would come with that shift.

HE: I am clear about the choice. So how is this working?

Wait! I think I know…. It's a work in progress.

SHE: Exactly.

Chapter 5: How THE PLAN showed up in the Middle Context

SHE: DU's Middles, like many Middles in organizations, are living in a tearing environment, torn between above and below and torn apart from one another.

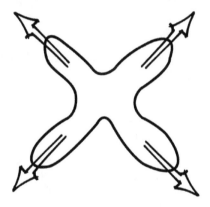

The Middle World is a tearing world

The more burdened Tops are, the more they look to Middles for help; and the more dissatisfied Workers are, the more they look to Middles to fix things. People are often looking to Middles for things Middles don't have; Tops may be looking to Middles for better quality, but Middles don't control quality; Workers may be looking to Middles for information Middles don't have and resources Middle don't control.

HE: You're describing my last job. Painful.

SHE: That's the point. It was your job but not just *your* job. This tearing is a worldwide context millions of Middles live in daily.

Constantly being torn between the conflicting needs, priorities, and demands of others.

This is the context in which DU's Middles are living. And into this tearing world comes THE PLAN.

HE: I can see what's coming. Tops are too overloaded so they look to Middles to deal with THE PLAN.

And Workers have no interest in implementing THE PLAN. So, Middles are stuck in the middle.

SHE: This is exactly what we were hearing from Middles. *Tops are too busy to deal with THE PLAN, so they look to me to handle it. The Workers are very skeptical about THE PLAN and they look to me for information and direction I don't have; and when I go to the Tops they don't have the answers I'm looking for; so, when I return empty-handed to the Workers... you can image the reception I get. And, of course, the Tops see me as lacking firm leadership.*

HE: So, in that Middle World, this wonderful PLAN showed up as just more tearing.

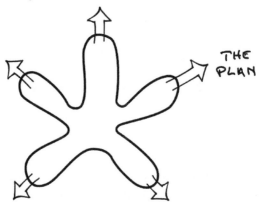

The Plan showing up in the Middle World as more tearing

SHE: Exactly. And what's happening to Middles functioning as the Integrating Mechanism of the system?

HE: My guess: Not happening.

SHE: Right again. Middles are totally tied up in their individual struggles.

The Middle Dance of Blind Reflex

SHE: It's in this tearing environment that it's easy for Middles to fall into the End/Middle/End Dance of Blind Reflex.

HE: Go slow. Middle I understand. What's an End?

SHE: Middles don't exist in isolation. There are always two or more Ends – individuals or groups – with their often conflicting needs and priorities, pulling Middles in different directions. The Tops are one End, the Workers another. Customers may be an End. Other Middles may be Ends.

Middle between multiple Ends

HE: OK. So, what's the End/Middle/End dance?

SHE: Middles, without awareness or choice, reflexively slide in between the Ends' issues and conflicts, and now *they* feel responsible for solving the Ends' issues and problems.

HE: Wait. Something I don't get.

SHE: Let me finish. And, what makes the Dance complete is that the Ends *also* hold Middles responsible. So, all are in agreement: Middles are responsible. And, if Middles fail, all are in agreement about that too. Middles are responsible. *Why did I get stuck with these weak, incompetent Middles?* Ah, such a perfect dance!

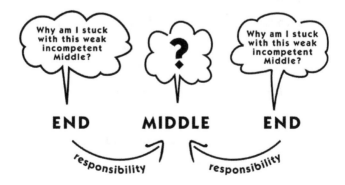

HE:	I'm not getting this "sliding in between."
SHE	Which may be why your last job was so painful.
HE:	I didn't *slide* in between, I *was* in between.
SHE:	And *you* felt responsible for resolving *their* issues. Right?
HE:	Of course; that was my job.
SHE:	Really? Think about it. Think about DU's Middles. They're in the middle of this mess regarding THE PLAN.
HE:	(Still defensive) In between.
SHE:	OK, in between. So, let me ask you a question. Did the Middles create this mess?
HE:	(Thinks) No.
SHE:	Who did?
HE:	(Ponders) Well, I suppose the first consulting group. They sold the Tops on THE PLAN.
SHE:	Anyone else?
HE:	I suppose the Tops. They're not giving THE PLAN the leadership it needs.
SHE:	Anyone else?
HE:	The Workers. They're fighting the whole thing.
SHE:	And what about the Middles?
HE:	They're stuck with all this. They don't know which way to turn.
SHE:	Don't you see? Not only are they stuck; *they are feeling responsible for resolving this issue.* And Tops and Workers are holding *them* responsible.
HE:	Which is exactly how I felt. Like it was all on me.
SHE:	*You* felt responsible for *their* issues.
HE:	Right.
SHE:	And *they* held you responsible for resolving *their* issues.
HE:	Right.
SHE:	And that is the Middle Dance of Blind Reflex.
HE:	Hmm. I need to think about this.

SHE: This sliding in between is not a conscious choice Middles make; it simply happens. It becomes crystal clear to Middles that *they* are responsible for resolving others' issues and problems. Once they slide, you can see how easy it is for Middles to become:

- weak, never fully satisfying some or all conflicting parties

- confused, not knowing what to believe

- self-doubting, because if you get enough negative feedback you begin to question your own competence.

HE: That's exactly what I was feeling.

SHE: You and millions of other Middles. And pay attention to this. This is a big one: It is an easy place for Middles to *lose their independence of thought and action.* All that matters is what *others* see and what *others* want. It's as if Middles don't have any unique perspective of their own. Which, of course, they do.

HE: What a picture. (starting to get angry) I feel responsible for resolving *their* issues. *They* hold *me* responsible for resolving *their* issues. All the time I'm worrying about *them*, taking *their* concerns into account, explaining them to one another, pleasing them. As if what I see has no value. As if I don't have a point of view.

SHE: I see by your tone that you're getting the rhythm of the Middle dance.

HE: And a feel for the work you needed to do with DU's Middles.

SHE: In THE PLAN, Middles are supposed to function as the Integrating Mechanism of the System. Meeting regularly with one another – sometimes face-to-face, sometimes virtually – sharing information, diagnosing system issues, coordinating system processes, seeing that Tops and Workers get the information and resources they need to do their work. So long as individual Middles fall into this torn condition, there is no possibility of their becoming part of DU's INTEGRATING MECHANISM.

HE: That's clear.

SHE: So, MICROSCOPE's work is to help the Middles see, understand, and master the tearing condition they're in. The work is to help

Middles recognize the Dance of Blind Reflex and what it costs them and the system.

HE: With the usual caution?

SHE: By now you know it.

HE: Whatever you do, don't tell Middles that they are torn *because* they slide in between others' issues and conflicts.

SHE: Exactly. There *is* considerable tearing built into the Middles' world. That's the reality they are living in. What the Middles need to see is how their sliding in between *increases* their tearing, and how that weakens them and diminishes the quality of their contributions to others and the system.

HE: Let's say they recognize the dance, then what?

SHE: The beginning place is *independence of thought and action.*

Middles needs to see that they are more than simply extensions of other people's needs, priorities, and agendas. They need to recognize their own unique perspective, and be willing to act on it.

HE: I'm not sure I get this yet.

SHE: Because you can't conceive of Middles having an independent perspective.

HE: It never occurred to me. *They*, the others, have perspectives, not us.

SHE: But Middles *do* have a perspective, and their perspective can be a uniquely productive one. Middles can soak in what others want and need, but ultimately they need to ask themselves *What do I see happening? What do I see the system needs now?*

HE: I need some examples.

SHE: Here's one. Top asks Middle to implement Top's new initiative. Sliding-in-between-Middle jumps to it and begins to implement Top's initiative, and it causes a mess. Middle-using-independent-thought-and-action takes a close look at Top's initiative, and, based on what she knows about the system, believes it will *not* play the way Top hopes it will play. In fact, it will have several negative consequences. So, rather than implementing it, she talks it over with Top, lays out what she sees as the negatives, and suggests a more workable approach. Top is then in a position to take more informed and effective action based on what Middles sees going on.

HE: It's about paying attention.

SHE: It's about valuing your unique perspective. And having the courage to act on it.

HE: Got it.

SHE: Here's another one. An oppressed Worker asks Middle to take a consistently ignored complaint to the Top and request immediate action. Sliding-in-between-Middle jumps to it and brings the complaint to the Top, and then gets caught up carrying messages back and forth between the two, explaining one party to the other, not quite doing enough to satisfy either party. Middle-using-independent-thought-and-action sees this issue as *their* issue, not his. He works with both Workers and Tops to set up a meeting between them for the purpose of resolving *their* issue.

HE: This could be tough medicine for Middles.

SHE: What are you seeing?

HE: This would be like a waiter telling you he's not going to bring you what you ordered because it would be bad for your health.

SHE: Now wouldn't *that* be an interesting development? But I do take your point. Independence does require saying NO when saying NO could be uncomfortable. So, Middle has to be ready to say YES to a more satisfying and more productive alternative.

HE: I'm seeing a theme here underlying MICROSCOPE's work, first with Tops, then Workers and now with Middles. Once you become aware of how context is influencing you, then comes the challenge of personal transformation: Tops, shifting from sucking up responsibility to creating responsibility, Workers, shifting from holding others responsible to being responsible, and now Middles, shifting from being the servants of others to being independent of others.

SHE: You have the pattern. And in this case, there is no end of potential transformative moments for Middles. Just at the point when the Dance of Blind Reflex is getting underway, just at that moment when you and others are colluding in holding you responsible

49

and them not responsible, to say "NO, this is not going to happen." *What is my perspective? What do I see happening? What does the system need from me now?*

HE: These are big shifts. Fundamental shifts.

SHE: Yes, they are. And I think you also see that these shifts are always in the service of the person *and* the system. That's what MICROSCOPE is all about: Seeing Self in System. Empowering both.

HE: And how is the work with DU's Middles going?

SHE: We're inviting them to explore a transformative alternative.

HE: Taking a stand on the kind of Middle you choose to be.

SHE: Exactly.

The Middle Empowerment Stand
In the presence of Middle Tearing,
a condition that will not go away,
instead of sliding in between others' issues and conflicts
and becoming the Torn Middle,
my stand is to be a Middle who maintains my
independence of thought and action in service of the system.

HE: This is not just a challenge for Middles, is it?

SHE: What are you seeing?

HE: A question: Does anyone want independent Middles?

SHE: An excellent question.

HE: And the answer is?

SHE: Only if they recognize the benefits for them and the system.

Chapter 6: How THE PLAN showed up in the Customer Context

HE: This should be interesting.

SHE: Painfully interesting.

In a world in which DU's Tops were sucking responsibility up to themselves and away from others and becoming burdened by increasing complexity, where Workers were holding THEM (Tops and Middles) responsible for things that were wrong with their condition and the condition of the system and becoming oppressed, where Middles were sliding in between others' issues and conflicts and becoming weak, confused, ineffective, it should come as no surprise that Customers were living in a world of NEGLECT: promises made, promises broken; products and services not coming to them when they wanted them, at the quality they expected, and at the price they wanted to pay. A customer survey made this very clear.

THE PLAN showing up in the Customer context as more neglect

Enter THE PLAN

HE: And into this world of neglect comes THE PLAN.

SHE: When the Customers first learned about the PLAN, they were enthusiastic. They had plenty of feedback for DU, as you can imagine, mostly negative. But they had little faith in the ability of the organization to use the feedback constructively.

HE: I can see it now. Feedback to the Tops is just more complexity, to the Middles it's more tearing, and to the Workers it just adds to their list of disregarded problems.

SHE: Yes, and there's something else. Being the system's Validator is more than giving the organization feedback; it's more than being angry; it's feeling like a *partner* of the organization, sharing responsibility for the organization's survival and development, being committed to its success. That aspect of Validating was totally absent.

HE: Given what was going on in DU, you'd have to be a saint to have that kind of commitment as a customer.

SHE: And it gets worse.

HE: The Dance of Blind Reflex?

SHE: Exactly.

The Customer Dance of Blind Reflex

SHE: In this environment of neglect it's easy for DU's Customers to fall into the Dance of Blind Reflex in which responsibility for delivery rests *solely* with DU's Providers and not with them. Provider responsible, Customer not responsible.

PROVIDER   **CUSTOMER**

Provider/Customer Dance

HE: Isn't that how it's supposed to be?

SHE: Maybe, but certainly not in THE PLAN. Just put yourself in the Customer position. It's crystal clear to you that the Provider is responsible for delivery, not you. Have you ever been there?

HE: Sure thing.

SHE: So, say you are getting good service. How are you feeling about the Provider?

HE: Like a satisfied customer. Happy. Grateful.

SHE: Probably you're not even noticing it; you're just taking good service for granted. That's how things are and ought to be. Are you feeling responsible for delivery?

HE: No. And I see where this is going. When delivery gets bad, I'm not feeling responsible for that either.

SHE: Exactly. So, when delivery is bad, it's crystal clear to you that *they* are responsible for delivery, not you. So *now* how are you feeling toward them?

HE: Angry. Upset. Blaming. Feeling let down.

SHE: And righteous?

HE: Righteous? Absolutely.

SHE: The righteously screwed Customer.

HE: I might have put it more delicately, but yes, that captures it.

SHE: And how committed are you now to the *company's* success?

HE: *Their success?* It's my success I'm worried about.

SHE: So, that's our work with DU's Customers. Once the Customer falls into the Dance of Blind Reflex, VALIDATING is no longer a possibility. The Customers aren't feeling responsible for DU's survival and growth. As far as they are concerned, survival is DU's business, not theirs. What Customers *are* concerned with is getting the service they feel entitled to and aren't getting.

HE: Better be quick before they are all gone.

SHE: You're right. Customer turnover is a big issue for DU. So, our work is to help Customers move past this righteous indignation and find personal satisfaction in being partners in DU's success.

HE: The joys of validating.

SHE: We have a way to go, but that's the work.

Caution!

HE: At least I know one way *not* to begin the work.

SHE: You're getting the message.

HE: Whatever you do, do not suggest to the Customer that the reason they are feeling righteously screwed is because they are holding DU responsible for delivery.

SHE: They have to know that we understand the reality of their situation. That there is good reason for their feelings. Delivery *is* unsatisfactory. What we want them to see is the costs the dance is exacting from *them*. And then to find a more satisfying and productive road ahead for them.

HE: You said: the costs for them, the Customers?

SHE: Think about it. Just what does holding DU responsible for delivery get the Customer?

HE: Well, it gets them a lot of righteousness.

SHE: Take that to the bank.

HE: It doesn't get you the service you want. I mean, it's not a very effective action strategy.

SHE: It's a poor strategy. It creates a vicious cycle. You get bad service to which you respond by holding them responsible which doesn't change bad service, in fact it makes you feel angrier, to which you respond by holding them responsible, and on and on it goes.

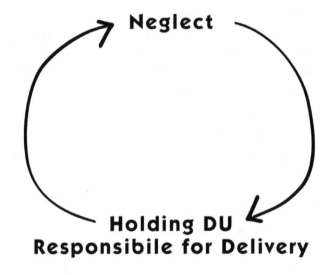

Holding DU responsible is not a good strategy for getting delivery

HE: Sometimes screaming does get results.

SHE: Sometimes, but screaming as a general customer practice also has its costs. Stress. Frustration. Rage. They take their toll.

And if there's value in creating an ongoing mutually satisfying and productive relationship with DU – which I think there is – this is not the best strategy for getting there.

HE: So, we need to help Customers recognize the costs the dance is exacting from them. Stress. Relationship. Poor Strategy for getting what they want.

SHE: All of that and something more fundamental. There is the matter of what is means to *be* customer. A choice.

HE: What do you mean?

SHE: It's a fundamental life issue for all of us. Are we the passive recipients of whatever life brings us, or are we active agents in shaping our lives? Do DU's Customers *choose* to be the passive recipients of whatever DU delivers or do they choose to be active agents in that process?

HE: So, our work with Customers is to help them shift from being the passive recipients of DU's services, to being active partners in delivery. That's a big shift.

SHE: That's a bit strong. At MICROSCOPE, we don't *help* people shift. Remember, our business is awareness and choice. We want Customers to see the current situation and their part in it. And then we are presenting a transformative alternative.

HE: You've said it before. Awareness is *our* business, choice is *theirs*.

SHE: That's the MICROSCOPE way.

HE: And the transformative alternative you're presenting to DU's Customers?

The Customer Empowerment Stand
In the presence of Customer Neglect,
a condition that will not go away,
instead of holding Dynamics Unlimited solely responsible for delivery,
and becoming the righteously screwed customer,
my stand is to be
a customer who works in partnership with Dynamics Unlimited,
Who shares responsibility for delivery,
Who stays connected to the delivery process
And helps it work for me.

HE: I sure can anticipate some resistance on this one. *I'm the Customer! Why am I responsible?*

SHE: Yes, and I can even hear the righteousness in *your* voice.

HE: It's tough to let that go.

SHE: Yes, it is. And would you like to know the secret to letting it go?

HE: Really. There *is* such a secret?

SHE: There is, and this is it. Live your life in the reality that *you are entitled to nothing.*

HE: Nothing?

SHE: Nothing. Try that on. No one owes you anything. Not Dynamics Unlimited. Not anyone. The *world* owes you nothing. Nothing you've done deserves anything. You do what you do. You get what you get. That is all there is. You aren't entitled to anything.

HE: Some secret. What do I do with it?

SHE: Just notice how liberating it is. How it frees you up from your hopes about what others will do, your expectations, your disappointments in what they do or don't do, your resentments.

You do what you do, the best you can, and get what you get.

HE: That's a mighty big one to let in.

SHE: I think you'll see just how liberating that will be.

HE: I am giving it my full consideration. One more thing. You're not going to tell Customers that getting poor delivery is just one more opportunity for personal growth, are you? You wouldn't do that, would you?

SHE: Actually we would. I'm *not* saying that Customers shouldn't be getting good service. They should, and that's our goal here. But what we are also saying is that disappointing service *will* happen. That's the way of life. And whenever that does happen, it *is* an opportunity for transformative growth. It's in those moments that the choice is present: Hold them responsible, fall into entitlement, becoming the angry, righteously screwed customer, withdrawing or lashing out, however you handle righteous anger. Or, stop, think, notice your reaction, let it pass. Say NO to the Dance of Blind Reflex, and say YES to what could be a more interesting, challenging, and personally transformative question: *How am I going to help this system work for me?*

HE: So, how's this working out?

SHE: Lots of interesting conversations happening.

*

57

Are we done here?

HE: I've put together a summary chart of MICROSCOPE's work with
Dynamics Unlimited. How does it look?

Summary of Work with Dynamics Unlimited

DU's Position	Immediate Context	Dance of Blind Reflex	Experience	Consequences for the PLAN	Required Transformation
Top	Complexity Accountability Uncertainty	Suck up responsibility	Burdened	Shaping Not Possible	**Be a Top who creates responsibility throughout the system**
Bottom	Vulnerability Problem Disregard	Hold Higher-Ups Responsible	Oppressed	Producing Not Possible	**Be a Worker who is responsible for my condition and for the condition of the whole**
Middle	Tearing	Slide in between others' issues and conflicts and make them your own	Torn	Integrating Not Possible	**Be a Middle who maintains my independence of thought and action in the service of the system**
Customer	Neglect	Hold the delivery system (DU) responsible for delivery	Righteously Screwed	Validating Not Possible	**Be a Customer who works in partnership with the delivery system**

SHE: Perfect… to a point.

HE: Am I missing something?

SHE: Do you remember the summary following the first attempts to implement THE PLAN?

HE: What I remember is that THE PLAN wasn't working.

SHE: It wasn't working because Tops were too burdened to SHAPE, oppressed Workers were not in any condition to PRODUCE, torn Middles couldn't INTEGRATE, and righteously screwed Customers had no interest in VALIDATING.

HE: And MICROSCOPE seems to be tackling those issues well, so are we done here?

SHE: Not quite. There was a second part to that summary.

The Summary Report: Part B

❖ *Tops are caught up in territoriality – defending, protecting, and embellishing their individual empires – and they are not inclined to work together as SHAPERS.*

❖ *Workers are unified but emotionally disengaged from the rest of the organization and, therefore, in no shape to function as PRODUCERS.*

❖ *Middles are totally alienated from one another; functioning together as the INTEGRATING MECHANISM is out of the question.*

Part II

Systems in Context

Chapter 7: Putting Whole Systems in Context

SHE: It's one thing to empower *individual* Tops, Middles, Workers, and Customers.

HE: That's no small accomplishment, and MICROSCOPE seems to be doing that well.

SHE: That's *part* of what we've been doing, but we understand that you don't transform systems one person at a time. *A thousand empowered leaders don't add up to one empowered system.*

HE: You seem exercised about this.

SHE: It's this cult of the individual. The hero who will save us. Just read the literature. It's about leaders: leaders with courage, character, flexibility, persistence, moral fiber, transparency, vulnerability, empathy, on and on it goes.

HE: But you do agree that those are important?

SHE: Important, but far from sufficient. Organizations are whole organic systems, and systems within systems. Transformation entails transforming whole systems. This means helping the members of each system see their system as a whole, in its immediate context, and help it master whatever challenges that context raises.

HE: Each system?

SHE: Dynamics Unlimited is a whole composed of three separate and interrelated systems. Top, Middle, and Bottom are distinct organic systems, each facing the unique challenges presented by its immediate context.

You've seen the costs when *individuals* are blind to the context they are in, *and* when they are blind to their reflexive responses to those contexts.

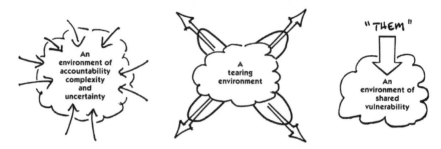

Three systems – Top, Middle, and Bottom – each in its own context

HE: Yes.

SHE: Well, whole systems face that same challenge. They can be blind to the contexts *they* are in, *and* blind to *their* reflexive responses to those contexts. That blindness is costly.

HE: And that's what happened at Dynamics Unlimited?

SHE: You saw the report. Good people. Well-intentioned. Talented. With all the possibilities of creating satisfying and productive partnerships with one another, instead fell into one version or another of internal warfare.

HE: And so MICROSCOPE's work was to help people see how all this happened and create those satisfying and productive partnerships? Sounds like a complex piece of work.

SHE: Yes, and I think by now you understand the essence of our approach.

HE: Awareness and choice.

SHE: We needed to start with basics. People are not accustomed to seeing, describing, or understanding, let alone mastering the whole systems they are in. We don't grasp the whole any better than the honey bee understands the Hive or the ant the Hill. We needed to begin by developing a common language we could use to describe the actions of Top, Middle, and Bottom systems. How do they interact with their environments? What is the whole-system equivalent of the Dance of Blind Reflex?

HE: We have such a language?

SHE: We do. The indispensable language of whole systems.

Chapter 8: The Indispensable Language of Whole Organic Systems

IND Individuation	INT Integration	DIF Differentiation	HOM Homogenization
Separate	Together	Differing	Commonality

SHE: Just as A,G,C,T[1] is an indispensable language for understanding the structure and processes of genes, so is the language we are introducing indispensable for understanding and mastering our whole system lives.

HE: All of them?

SHE: All of them, from your family to General Electric.

HE: That's quite a spread!

SHE: What differentiates one organic system from another is *balance* (which processes are predominant and which are submerged), *intensity* (how zestfully or anemically these processes are expressed), and awareness *(whether these are blind, reflexive responses or conscious intentional choices.)*

HE: Balance, intensity, and consciousness. That's all that's needed to understand whole organic systems?

SHE: Maybe not all, but they will serve us well.

---

[1] *A, C, G,* and *T,* representing the four nucleotide bases of a DNA strand — adenine, cytosine, guanine, thymine.

HE: Wow, that's overwhelming. I'm afraid I need a bit more detail.

SHE: So did the people at Dynamics Unlimited. So, we began with the basics. What whole systems do.

What Do Whole Systems Do?

I. Individuation and Integration

SHE: To understand whole systems you'll need to adopt the position of the observer, the one who stands apart from whole systems and notices what they are doing.

HE: Like observing the movement of bees as they dance around the hive.

SHE: Exactly. Only now you are standing apart and observing your own family as a whole system, or your work team, or the divisions in an organization, or the nations of the world. And here's what you'll notice.

Whole systems INDIVIDUATE, with the parts – individuals and groups – operating independently of one another, going their own way, doing their own thing, functioning as independent wholes.

And whole systems INTEGRATE, with the parts functioning together as interdependent components of a larger whole.

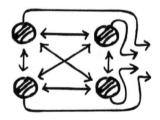

Apart, together. Separate, connected. Independent, interdependent.

HE: OK, simple enough. My family, for example. Most of the time we are individuating, each of us is off doing his and her own thing, and sometimes, too rarely, we are integrating, like when we come together, say, to plan a vacation or a meal. Individuating and integrating.

SHE: Fine. Now can you also stand apart and observe your university as a whole system and see all its departments as the parts? Can you observe that whole system individuating and integrating?

HE: I get it. So, individuation is not just about individuals. It's about the parts of the whole, whether the parts are individuals or groups.

SHE: Or religions, or nations. For example, visualize the nations of the world as being parts of a single system comprising all the nations of the world.

HE: Individual nations as parts of the whole? Interesting.

SHE: And notice those parts individuating and integrating.

HE: What I'm noticing in all these cases is that some parts may be integrated with certain parts of the whole but not with others.

SHE: Right. And there are all sorts of variations. But for now our business is simply to get comfortable with the language. This is the DNA of whole systems. Think about it as the alphabet, the A, B, Cs. Later on we'll use this simple alphabet to unravel mysteries, reveal possibilities, and fundamentally transform system life.

HE: For Dynamics Unlimited?

SHE: For all organic systems.

HE: You have my interest.

SHE: So let's continue.

What Do Whole Systems Do?

II. Differentiation and Homogenization

SHE: Whole systems DIFFERENTIATE. They develop specialized forms and functions. The parts of the system elaborate their differences from one another, with each part serving its specialized function.

And whole systems HOMOGENIZE, with the parts developing or maintaining their commonality with one another, sharing common information, knowledge, and capacity.

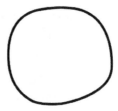

HE: Difference and commonality. They seem fundamental.

SHE: That they are. Of the two, differentiation is the easier to observe. Evidence is all around us.

HE: Isn't the human organism a classic study in differentiation? We begin life as this single-cell organism and in a matter of months we develop into this incredibly complex organism of systems within systems: respiratory, digestive, muscular, cardiovascular, et cetera, et cetera. And each organ or process is specialized, different from the others.

SHE: Right. And if you go into business, the business entity soon differentiates, developing different structures and processes –

production, marketing, sales, staffing, finance. And as the business grows, even these functions differentiate.

HE: Food preparation is another good example. I visualize primitive man; he hunts, he heats (maybe), he eats. Now, look at how food preparation has evolved and continues to evolve into this incredible variety of cuisines and manners of preparation.

SHE: Spiritual quests differentiate. Language has differentiated and continues to differentiate.

HE: Sports teams. Attack and defense, and then differentiations within each in terms of strategies and tactics.

SHE: The same for the military. Attack. Defense. Strategies and tactics. Weaponry. On and on, example after example. Whole systems continuing to differentiate, to develop variety in form and function.

HE: OK, ok. Differentiation is everywhere, and we could go on endlessly. But talk to me now about homogenization, the one you said is less easy to observe.

SHE: Difficult to observe, which may be why its critical importance is so often overlooked. First let me add something. When I described differentiation, your first image was the human organism.

HE: Yes, I could see that.

SHE: So let's observe a very different organism, the flatworm. If you cut certain species of flatworm horizontally in half, a strange thing happens. The head half develops a new tail, and the tail half develops a new head.

HE: That's fascinating.

SHE: That's homogenization. The information needed to create heads and tails is spread *throughout* the flatworm system.

HE: And that's not true of the human body. Cut us in half and we don't develop new heads...

SHE: Or tails.

HE: So this is essence of homogenization. It is the process by which system information, knowledge, and capacity are spread throughout the system.

SHE: And in the ultimate homogenized system, any part of the system can perform the function of any other part of the system.

HE: Let's see if I get it. When systems differentiate, each part develops its own specialized knowledge which is not available to other parts of the system; and when they homogenize, the system's knowledge, information, capacity is spread through the system.

SHE: That's it, basically.

HE: One question, and I think I already know the answer. It is possible, isn't it, for a system to be *both* differentiated *and* homogenized?

SHE: You are touching on a critical issue of system life. When we return to the Dynamics Unlimited story, you will see just how important your question is.

But basically the answer is: yes, it is possible...to *an extent.* You can also see how differentiated information can be so complex that it would make homogenization of that information throughout the system difficult or impossible.

HE: Understood. One more question. Are you saying whole systems *want to* perform these functions or that they *can*? I'm not clear.

SHE: I'm simply saying that this is what they *do.* Think of your breathing. Is breathing something you do because you *choose to?* Of course not; it's a bodily process. It is something your organism *does.* That is all we are doing here. Whole systems individuate, integrate, differentiate, and homogenize. That's what they do.

HE: The image of breathing helps.

SHE: Let's stay with it a bit longer. Most of the time you are unaware of your breathing, yet aware or unaware your body continues to breathe. Sometimes your breathing is calm and steady, and sometimes it *reflexively* becomes more intense when, for example, you are running or climbing stairs or are frightened. Sometimes you are aware of your breathing and are able to control the depth, timing, and length of breaths. So you can see the variety of forms your organism's breathing can take – aware or unaware, reflexive or mindful, intense or calm. But, what's the one thing your organism cannot do?

HE: Stop breathing?

70

SHE: Exactly. Because breathing is what your system does.

HE: And the same can be said for these processes of whole systems?

SHE: Exactly. These are what whole systems do. And, like breathing, they happen with variations in balance, intensity, and blind reflex or conscious choice.

HE: Ok so far, I think I'm getting it.

SHE: Let's see. Try this. Think about a system that is highly individuated with little or no integration. What's happening?

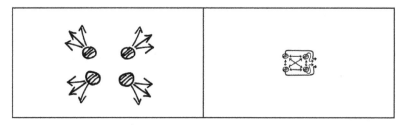

HE: There could be anarchy, chaos. It's not much of a system. People off doing their own things. And no collective action.

SHE: Right. Try this: Highly integrated, very little individuation.

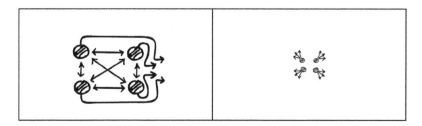

HE: Hmm. It feels stifling. No freedom. Too much togetherness.

SHE: You're getting the idea. What about highly differentiated, no homogenization?

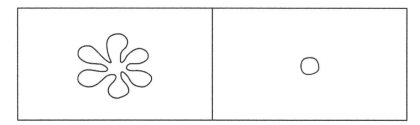

HE: Silos. I've seen lots of that. Lots of specialties with very little sharing or communicating or cooperation across boundaries. University departments come to mind. Organization functions too.

SHE: And total homogenization, with no differentiation?

HE: Hmm. I guess there'd be lots of shared knowledge, skills, and beliefs. Replaceable parts, and no indispensable members. Lots of unity, but a limited repertoire for engaging with the environment. Like that flatworm.

SHE: Good. You're grasping the basics, and you can see how there are infinite variations.

HE: But I'm still confused.

Confusion: Individuation and Differentiation

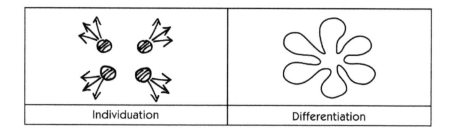

HE: Help me understand the difference between individuation and differentiation. I get confused

SHE: What's your question?

HE: As I'm understanding it, individuation has the parts – individuals or groups – operating separately from one another, going their own way. But here's my question. As the parts go their own way, don't they also become more different from one another? Isn't that differentiation?

SHE: Not necessarily. Say you have one hundred workers on the factory floor. All of them have the identical job – driving bolts into a body frame – and all of them are operating separately from one another. Or maybe you have ten groups of workers, and all groups have the same identical job.

In both cases – 100 individuals or 10 groups – these are individuated systems, the parts operating separately from one another, but each entity is performing the *same* function. Is either of these a differentiated system?

HE: No, I guess not.

SHE: And what do you think a differentiated system would look like?

HE: It could be something like a system composed of ten groups, where one group bolts, another paints, another assembles, and another polishes. One system with multiple functions.

SHE: Exactly. And say you had just one group, and that one group bolted, painted, assembled, and polished.

HE: I suppose that one group would still be a differentiated system.

SHE: And say you had one person who performed all those functions.

HE: One person as a differentiated system?

SHE: Why not? Differentiation has nothing to do with the number of system parts – individuals or groups – or whether they are together or apart. It only has to do with the number and type of specialized functions the system performs.

HE: OK. I think I have it.

Confusion: Integration and Homogenization

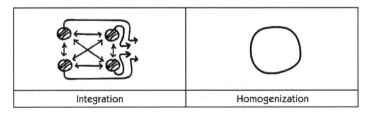

| Integration | Homogenization |

SHE: I suppose there's also this confusion between integration and homogenization.

HE: Now that you mention it.

SHE: Let's take a look.

HE: It's the same question in a way. As the parts integrate – coming together, interacting with one another – isn't the system homogenizing? Aren't the parts sharing common information, capacity, et cetera?

SHE: Your apparent confusion reveals an important understanding of the connection between these processes.

HE: That could make me feel a little better about myself.

SHE: As long as you understand that individuation and differentiation are different processes, and that integration and homogenization are also different processes, then it's possible to see how they are *both* different *and* connected.

HE: Please explain.

SHE: If system parts – members or groups – are integrating, it is possible that, as a consequence of that process, they begin to develop mutual understanding, shared knowledge, information and capacity.

HE: So, integration and homogenization are not the same processes, but they are connected. *By integrating we may come to experience our shared commonality.*

SHE: Exactly. And do you see how that also holds true for individuation and differentiation?

HE: Let me see. Individuation is about being separate, apart. And differentiation is about being different. So the question is: does being apart increase the likelihood of our growing more different from one another? And I see how it can.

SHE: Even our ten identical work groups, working separately from one another, might eventually develop different approaches to work, different ways of organizing, different processes.

HE: Individuation – being separate from one another – can lead to our growing different from one another.

SHE: *Can* is the operative word.

HE: Got it.

A brief but significant interlude

HE: Can I slow this lesson down a bit?

SHE: Of course.

HE: This conversation is not just theoretical; it seems to me to have immense societal implications.

SHE: What are you seeing?

HE: Take these last two points.

First. *Individuation can stimulate differentiation.* How our being separate from one another can enable our differences to grow. Where is *that* not playing out in society? The distance and corresponding tension between social classes. Out of touch with one another and growing more different from one another. The same with identity issues connected with immigration and the changing complexion of societies. How staying separate and apart supports the growth of our differences.

And then there's the second item. *Integration supports homogenization.* How our connecting can increase our experience of commonality. I'm thinking about all the possibilities that insight could open up for understanding and resolving societal issues.

SHE: I'm with you. There are important implications.

HE: What's most striking to me is that you are not laying these out as moral principles. It's not about being good or bad people. And you're not giving advice. You are simply illuminating how the *pattern* of whole-system processes has predictable consequences for how we experience and relate to one another. There is something both troubling and exciting in understanding this, that our experiences of one another are not as rock-solid as we'd like to believe. *I feel the way I feel about you or your group not because of who you are but because we are apart, and if we integrated in some meaningful way I would feel very differently about you or your group.* I think I'm really beginning to get to the depth of this.

SHE: Hold onto that experience. There's more to come.

HE: I'm ready.

Choosing Robust Systems

HE: It seems to me that we've talked primarily about the four processes and the consequences when systems are in or out of balance. But earlier you also talked about intensity and consciousness.

SHE: Yes. Let's explore those. Generally, we are unaware of these processes of the whole. We simply go about our business, and our systems run the risk of blindly and reflexively falling into dysfunctional patterns. We saw ample examples of that in DU's Top, Middle, and Bottom systems. But, once we understand these processes, it is possible for us to become mindful about them. We can choose. How individuated are we? How integrated? How differentiated? How homogenized? And, with consciousness or mindfulness, it becomes possible to transform reflexive and anemic systems into Robust Systems. And that was the possibility we saw for Dynamics Unlimited. To develop Top, Middle, and Bottom systems that are balanced and robust.

HE: As opposed to unbalanced and anemic.

SHE: Exactly. This means that all four processes are being expressed and elaborated intentionally, fully and completely. Zestfully. No compromise. All out.

HE: What would that look like?

SHE: Top, Middle, and Bottom systems are zestfully individuating. In each system, all members are not just operating independently, they are using themselves fully, risking, experimenting, going all out. They're identifying and using their unique potentials in the service of *their* system.

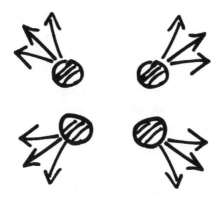

A Robust System zestfully individuating

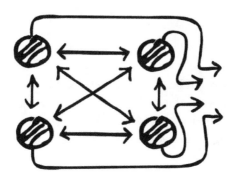

A Robust System zestfully integrating

And *each system is zestfully integrating*. Members within each system are regularly joining together in various configurations, working together, actively sharing information, feeding and supporting one another, coaching one another in the service of whatever enterprises they are working on.

HE: Zestfully apart *and* zestfully together. Back and forth. Out and in.

SHE: That's the pattern.

And while that's happening, each whole system is zestfully differentiating, developing and pursuing a variety of forms and functions for achieving its mission, for coping with the dangers it is facing and prospecting among the opportunities. Each system adopts promising new approaches and sheds forms that are no longer serving it well. Each system changes form and function in response to changing environmental conditions: new opportunities to grasp, new dangers to deal with.

A Robust System zestfully differentiating

HE: Differentiation helps me see these as living things, constantly taking in new information, changing, adapting. I can visualize an organization reacting to a changing competitive field, a business struggling to survive and grow, a government concerned with security.

SHE: Yes, and while that's happening, each system is *zestfully homogenizing*. Information, knowledge, expertise, new developments are actively shared across the system.

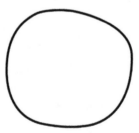

A Robust System zestfully homogenizing

HE: The other three processes are more intuitive for me. Homogenization, not so much. In fact, homogenization tends to have a negative connotation, doesn't it? *The world is becoming too homogenized, we're losing the richness of difference. One identical strip mall after another.*

SHE: I understand that. At the same time, it's important to see homogenization as the latent powerhouse process, the world-changer. I don't have to give you the details of a world in which differentiation – of religion, ethnicity, class, politics, nationalism – reigns supreme, while homogenization remains quiescent.

HE: I get your point. Homogenization to the rescue!

SHE: Only sometimes.

HE: *Only sometimes.* Of course. Revolutions have been known to swap one form of imbalance for another. Differentiation without homogenization causes one kind of problem. And societies that have attempted homogenization without differentiation have created their own kind of crushing oppression and suffering.

SHE: Always in the name of some misguided ideology. We will get to that at some later date, but now we need to complete our seminar on whole-system processes.

HE: Where to now?

SHE: Love and power.

HE: You're kidding.

SHE: Not really.

Love and Power: The Yin and Yang of Organic Systems

SHE: We've been viewing the four building blocks as processes in tension with one another: Individuation – separateness – is in tension with Integration – togetherness.

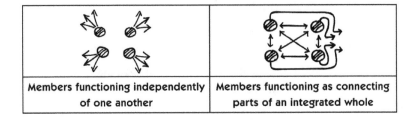

| Members functioning independently of one another | Members functioning as connecting parts of an integrated whole |

Differentiation – difference – is in tension with Homogenization – sameness.

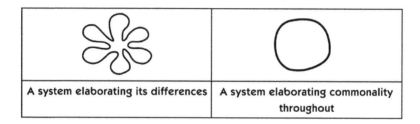

A system elaborating its differences	A system elaborating commonality throughout

As we'll see, in day-to-day system life, these processes tend to function in different configurations.

Individuation and differentiation tend to operate together,

You can think of this combination (individuation + differentiation) as the system's Power processes.

Parts operating independently of one another. Parts elaborating their difference from other parts. Together these express the *outgoing* aspect of systems.

And integration and homogenization tend to operate together.

You can think of this combination (integration + homogenization) as the system's Love processes.

Parts connecting with one another. Parts elaborating their commonality with one another. Together these express the *inward* aspect of systems.

HE: It's a bit unusual to talk about systems expressing power and love.

SHE: Unusual maybe, but that doesn't make it wrong. You and I are whole systems. Each of us expresses our power by individuating and differentiating, operating independently of others and establishing our difference from others. And each of us expresses our love by connecting with others and experiencing our commonality with them.

HE: I can see that. Persons express Love and Power. But organizations? That will take some getting used to.

SHE: It will, and our goal at Microscope is to have many more people getting used to it because it will serve all of us well.

HE: OK.

SHE: And once we recognize systems as expressing Power and Love, we can now visualize the full potential of Robust Systems, whether the system is you or me, or a group, an organization, nation, or world.

Robust Systems zestfully express their Love and Power.

Robust Systems express their Power by zestfully unleashing the full potential of system members, turning them loose to become all that *they* can be, and they express their Power by zestfully differentiating, elaborating *the system's* potential, becoming all that *it* can be.

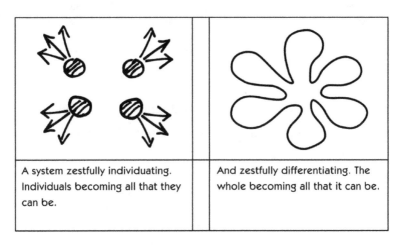

| A system zestfully individuating. Individuals becoming all that they can be. | And zestfully differentiating. The whole becoming all that it can be. |

A Robust System expressing its Power

HE: System Power. Zestful individuating combined with zestful differentiating. I feel the power, movement, energy and growth.

SHE: Exactly. And whole systems express their Love by zestfully integrating, with members working together in common cause, sharing with one another, supporting one another, and they express their Love by zestfully homogenizing, elaborating their commonality of information, knowledge, expertise, purpose, their unity, their one-ness.

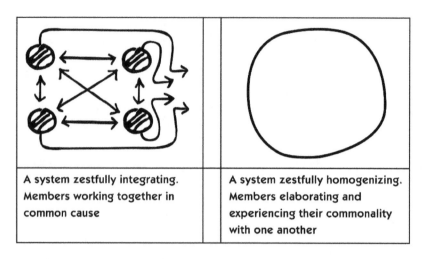

| A system zestfully integrating. Members working together in common cause | A system zestfully homogenizing. Members elaborating and experiencing their commonality with one another |

A Robust system expressing its Love

HE: Power and Love. It feels like such a fundamental distinction.

SHE: Power and Love *is* the story of Dynamics Unlimited.

HE: Please elaborate.

SHE: In a nutshell:

DU's Tops have fallen into a pattern of Power without Love.

DU's Workers have fallen into a pattern of Love in relationship to one another, and Power in relationship to the rest of the organization.

And DU's Middles have fallen into a pattern of neither Power nor Love.

And nobody is aware of how all of this has happened.

And, if these patterns were to persist, THE PLAN would just be words on paper.

Tops wouldn't be able to function as system SHAPERS.

Workers wouldn't be system PRODUCERS.

And Middles wouldn't be system INTEGRATORS.

HE: I'll be fascinated to see how MICROSCOPE unravels this.

SHE: That's up next. But, first let's summarize what we've established so far.

The Indispensable Language of Whole Systems

Summary

IND Individuation	INT Integration	DIF Differentiation	HOM Homogenization
Separate	Together	Differing	Commonality

- ❖ All whole organic systems individuate, integrate, differentiate, and homogenize.

- ❖ Systems vary in the balance of these processes and the intensity and mindfulness with which they are expressed.

- ❖ Robust systems are systems whose energy comes from the zestful expression of all four processes.

- ❖ Systems express their Power potential by mindfully and zestfully individuating and differentiating.

- ❖ Systems express their Love potential by mindfully and zestfully integrating and homogenizing.

- ❖ And most importantly: All systems – Top, Middle, Bottom – have the potential for being Robust systems, systems of Power and Love.

*

HE: I gather *potential* is the key word.

SHE: Yes, because when we are blind to context, we regularly fall out of that potential, as we saw at Dynamics Unlimited.

HE: So, whole systems have *their* dance of blind reflex.

SHE: They do.

HE: And that is what was happening at Dynamics Unlimited?

SHE: At Dynamics Unlimited and at endless numbers of organizations.

HE: And our work at MICROSCOPE?

SHE: The usual. To convert blindness to sight. Awareness and choice.

HE: I'm eager to see how this is working.

SHE: Coming up. But first you need to understand something. We were dealing with deeply held feelings throughout DU. One would expect strong resistance to changing relationships, some of which were fraught with misunderstanding and animosity. We needed a strategy to unfreeze experiences that felt so real and solid.

HE: And that strategy is?

Chapter 9: MICROSCOPE's Strategy

"This story is not about you…"

SHE: That summary report was the tip of the iceberg. Teamwork at DU was, at best, an aspiration unconnected with reality. Bad feelings among the Tops had been intensifying over time. Middles didn't particularly like or respect one another, and there was lingering resentment among some Middles at having been undermined by others. And as the report showed, Workers had become increasingly disenchanted with and disengaged from the rest of the organization.

    Here is the main point. *All of these experiences were felt to be real and solid and specific to these particular people. "I feel the way I feel about you because that's the reality of who you are."*

HE: Isn't that obvious?

SHE: Obvious maybe, but not true. And that's the point. The *very big point.* These dramas at DU are not just about these particular people. They have to see that. What was happening at DU was what happens with great regularity to Top, Middle, and Bottom systems elsewhere.

HE: So people are taking personally issues that are not personal. They go with the territory.

SHE: And once you *deeply* understand the territory, you can change the experience. That's the heart of this work.

HE: So how did you proceed?

SHE: We avoided dealing directly with DU's issues. We simply shared powerful knowledge about human systems. Over time, we've developed educational presentations describing familiar Top,

Middle, and Bottom system stories. These are what we share. We make it clear to each group we're presenting to: *The story we are about to share with you is not about you, and not about Dynamics Unlimited. This is a story about [Top, Middle, or Bottom] systems generally. If you see connections between the story and your experience at DU, that's fine. We'll work with that.*

HE: I get it.

*

Top, Middle, and Bottom System Stories

What follows are selected slides and commentary from MICROSCOPE's presentations as they were made to members of DU's Top, Middle, and Bottom systems.

Chapter 10: The Annotated Slide Show For Tops

A Tale of Top Systems

Commentary: *This is a story of a potentially Robust Top system, a system with outstanding capacity to deal with the challenges and opportunities it is facing.*

Here is how it begins

A talented collection of People

Commentary: Enter the members of the Top system. This is a talented, well-intentioned group of people, committed to the organization's mission and its success. This group has been brought together because it was felt that they would make a great top team.

SHE: But pay attention to this. This sense of their unique potential plays an important part in the Top story. Generally, people are brought together in the Top space because it's thought that they will create a great team. Either it's their complementary expertise, or their prior experiences with one another, or their love for one another.

HE: Love? Love among the Tops?

SHE: Love may not have been a factor for DU's Tops, but remember, there are all sorts of Top contexts in the world. Think about it: contexts in which people are collectively responsible for a system characterized by complexity and uncertainty, *and* where love, or at least friendship, is what has drawn them together.

HE: Like parents in the family? As a parent with children, a mortgage, car payments, decisions about their futures and ours, it feels like a Top context. Complexity, uncertainty, and accountability.

SHE: Clearly a Top context, and one in which, I assume, you came together out of love.

HE: Absolutely. As the slide says, *What a great group this is.*

SHE: So, this slide show will have relevance for you, for all parents who came together out of love, for business partners who came together because they were siblings, for partners who were great friends in college. *So why not continue the good times in business?*

HE: I see the point. We've experienced each other in one context, and now we're moving into another very different context. What we're focused on is our feelings for one another. What we're not paying attention to is *context.*

SHE: There's a bright future for you at MICROSCOPE. This new Top context has the potential for fundamentally changing these relationships. And since those relationships may have begun in mutual respect, admiration, friendship, and love, their deterioration, if it happens, will be an especially bitter pill to swallow.

The Top context heats up

Commentary: *The Top system is engaging with an environment of complexity, uncertainty, and accountability. Lots of issues to deal with, complex issues, issues for which there are no simple clear-cut answers. Business as usual will no longer suffice. New strong competition is emerging; a changing workforce demographic is creating new pressures; existing technology is becoming obsolete; government policies are in flux. The Top system is in danger of being overwhelmed by complexity.*

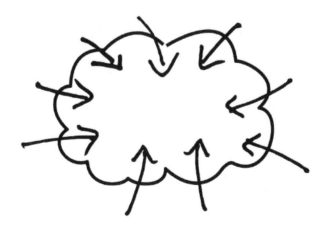

Top system in an environment of complexity, accountability, and uncertainty

SHE: Here we see the Top system not as a collection of individuals but *as a whole organic* entity engaging with this environment, and we observe how that whole reacts to these conditions.

HE: This may be hard for people to really grasp. As you've said before, we see people, we don't see this whole.

SHE: That's true, and that is why we keep falling into the same dysfunctional scenarios. The whole point of these presentations is to help people see, understand, and master the *wholes* of which we are a part.

HE: Understood.

SHE: Let's watch.

The Top system adapts

Commentary: *The Top system reflexively adapts by differentiating.*

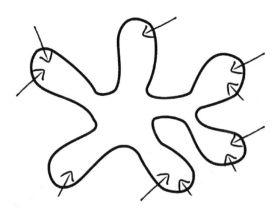

Top system differentiating

Different individual Tops or groups of Tops assume responsibility for different elements of the complexity. Differentiation is an adaptive response; it allows the Top system to begin to cope with the complexity and accountability it is facing, to not be overwhelmed by it. Differentiation is not the problem. What happens next is.

Sclerosis sets in

Commentary: Without awareness or choice, differentiations harden into territories, processes continuing to move in the direction they are already moving.

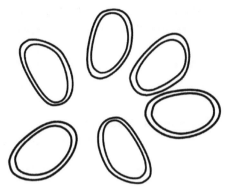

Differentiations harden into separate territories

HE: Why does this happen?

SHE: Keep in mind that all of this is occurring without awareness or choice. Reflex. The whole reacts, and the whole continues to evolve in the direction it is evolving.

HE: A whole-systems version of inertia.

SHE: Sounds right.

The Top systems become differentiated and individuated

Commentary: Territories grow more differentiated and individuated, more distinct from one another and operating increasingly independently of one another. Tops burrow down into their respective territories, becoming increasingly knowledgeable about, responsible for, and committed to their territories, and decreasingly knowledgeable about, responsible for, and committed to the territories of others.

Territoriality: Power without Love

Commentary: *The Top system has fallen out of the possibility of being a Robust system and into an unbalanced and anemic territorial pattern, a system of Power without Love.*

The parts – territories – have grown more different from one another – more specialized – and they are operating increasingly separately from one another.

Differentiation and individuation predominate while homogenization and integration are submerged.

Territorial Pattern

Dominant Processes Power	Submerged Processes Love
Differentiation	Homogenization
Individuation	Integration

A crucial piece of system knowledge:
The patterns systems fall into
shape the consciousness of system members.

Commentary: *Once a system falls into a pattern, that pattern shapes how members experience themselves, others, their system, and other systems. And then members behave consistently with that consciousness.*
All of this happens without awareness or choice.

SHE: This is a fundamental insight into ourselves as systems creatures: how our consciousness is at the mercy of the patterns we have blindly fallen into.

HE: So, I hate you not because you're hateful, but because of the pattern we have fallen into?

SHE: Sounds ridiculous, doesn't it?

HE: Sort of.

SHE: Yet it is often true, and that is a very difficult truth to accept.

Let's see how this plays out in the Top context.

Power without Love results in A "Mine" consciousness

Commentary: As the Top system becomes more differentiated and individuated, with Tops burrowing down into their respective territories, members fall into a "mine" mentality, becoming protective and defensive of their territories. Their behavior then reflects that mentality, burnishing their territories and acting in protective and defensive ways. For example, preventing other Tops from interfering in their business, sharing information that puts their territory in a positive light, and withholding information that doesn't.

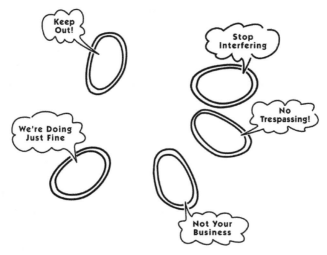

Tops fall into a "Mine" mentality

A vicious cycle develops

Commentary: *The "mine" mentality leads Tops to take actions – protecting and defending their territories. Those actions reinforce the territorial structure they are in, and that structure reinforces the "mine" mentality, and on and on it goes.*

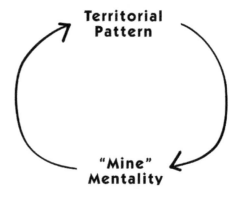

This vicious cycle serves to solidify the territorial structure, making it resistant to change.

Relationship issues among Tops unfold

Commentary: *Tops become vulnerable to certain relationship tensions and breakdowns. It is important to note that these relationship issues are the natural consequences of the "Power without Love" pattern that Tops have fallen into. They go with the pattern.*

*Members of the Top system are vulnerable to falling into issues around **relative significance**: who are the more and less important members in the Top team? There may be issues around **respect**: Tops feeling that they are not getting from other Tops the respect they deserve for their contributions. There may be issues around **trust**: members counting on other members to carry out their responsibilities, and not trusting that they do. There may be issues around **support**: members feeling that they are not getting the support they need from other Tops; in fact, feeling undermined by them. There is much finger-pointing and blame, spoken or unspoken.*

SHE: Keep in mind that these people came together as Tops because they were well matched, and because they respected and liked one another. And now, look at what has happened to these special relationships.

HE: I've seen all of this played out in business partnerships. They began in promise and ended in disaster. All of these issues: relative significance, respect, trust, support. Bitterness.

SHE: And marriages?

HE: There too.

Systemic issues unfold

Commentary: *Tops in their differentiated/individuated territories tend to create territorial silos throughout the system resulting in the build-up of redundant and costly resources, conflicting and confusing messages being sent through the system, system members torn by conflicting loyalties, important information getting lost in the cracks, loss of potential cross-system synergies, and the Top territoriality reinforcing the dis-integration of the middle of the organization.*

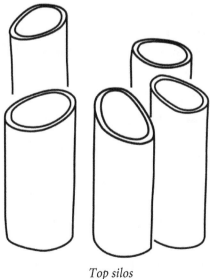

Top silos

Without awareness or choice

Commentary: *Whatever happened to that talented, committed group whose members had the potential to become a Robust Top system? They have fallen into a dysfunctional territorial pattern, a pattern of Power without Love. The consequence: individual stress, broken, non-cooperative, conflictive relationships, organizational disintegration, lost opportunities, diminished contributions, finger pointing and blame; and all of this happens without awareness of how their own blind reflexive behavior has brought all of this about.*

HE: I'll be interested to learn how DU's Tops reacted to the presentation, but first I have a question. You talked about this territorial pattern being unbalanced and anemic. I can see clearly that it's unbalanced, but how is it anemic?

SHE: Sure. Differentiation is the key process for the survival and success of the Top system. The Top system needs *robust* differentiation. It needs to be able to continuously reshape itself in response to changing environmental circumstances. It needs to be able to develop new differentiations to deal with emerging dangers and opportunities, and be able to discard differentiations that are no longer functional. So, I ask you: Is that the type of differentiation that you've seen in this dance?

HE: Hardly.

SHE: What *do* you see?

HE: The system has fallen into a differentiated form and rigidified in *that* form. That's a far cry from the fluid form of differentiation you're describing.

SHE: That's right. It's not as if the whole Top system is working together to master differentiation. It's stuck.

HE: Unbalanced, sclerotic, *and* anemic. A very weak form of differentiation.

SHE: And mastering differentiation is at the heart of SHAPING. So long as Tops are mired in territoriality, SHAPING can't happen.

HE: I can see that. SHAPING involves Tops working *together* to identify the emerging dangers and opportunities in the system's environment.

SHE: So, our challenge has been to help Tops see their current condition, to recognize how it got to where it is, and then to choose a healthier, more satisfying, and productive alternative.

HE: To move from unbalanced, sclerotic, and anemic to balanced and robust. A Top system of Power *and* Love.

SHE: That's the goal.

With Awareness comes Choice,

Creating Robust Top Systems

The "solution" is obvious

Dominant Power Processes	Submerged Love Processes
Differentiation	Homogenization
Individuation	Integration

Territorial Pattern

Systemic awareness

HE: Looking at this Territoriality chart, you can see what needs to be done.

It's like a cooking recipe. Add a bit of Love – homogenization and integration – to the mix and the Top system will be whole again.

SHE: It will take more than a "bit" of Love, but that *is* the general direction. Tops are suffering from a commonality/ connectedness deficit.

They've grown more different from one another, and have lost their experience of commonality.

They've grown more separate from one another, and have lost their connectedness.

So, Tops need to bring Love – Integration and Homogenization – into play, *and to do it in a way that strengthens Power – Individuation and Differentiation.*

HE: That's interesting. So, it's not a matter of toning down Power; it's about strengthening both.

SHE: Exactly.

But none of that was going to happen so long as Tops were stuck in their "Mine" mentality. Their focus would be to go on protecting, defending, and enhancing *their* territories. Strategies that, based on our chart, seemed reasonable and promising, in *their* world would likely have been experienced as impractical and dangerous.

HE: So your goal was to use the Dance of Blind Reflex presentation to get them out of the "Mine" mentality.

SHE: Right, to help them shift from a personal perspective to a systemic one.

HE: Please spell that out for me.

A Fundamental Shift in Perspective

From Personal	To Systemic
Specific. Our experiences feel like they're specific to these particular people and circumstances.	**Patterns.** What we're experiencing is a pattern, one that occurs regularly in systems like ours.
Reality. How we experience ourselves and others feels like a reflection of who we and they *really* are.	How we experience ourselves and others is a consequence of the pattern we have fallen into. What we see is not all there is.
Change. Change comes by fixing the people, ourselves and others.	Change the pattern, and our experience of the people will change.

SHE: The shift is from feeling that their experiences of one another are specific to these particular Tops and their circumstances, to seeing that what they are experiencing is a *regularly recurring pattern*, one that is common to Top systems engaging with environments of complexity, uncertainty, and accountability.

The shift is from believing their experiences are a reflection of reality (that what they see and feel is what is), to recognizing that their experiences are a *consequence* of the territorial pattern they've fallen into.

The shift is from believing that the solution to their relationship difficulties, if there is one, is to change the people – fix, fire, rotate, separate, send off for therapy – to seeing that the solution lies in changing the pattern they have fallen into.

HE: That is one huge shift. Our experiences feel so real, so solid.

SHE: You're right, of course. Yet, if we are ever to get out of our endless destructive scenarios, that is the shift we humans need to make.

HE: I understand that. So, did the Tops make that shift?

SHE: They did the best you could hope for. They expressed a willingness to explore. What would it look like to infuse Love – homogenization and integration - into Power? What forms would it take? So that's what we explored with them.

Infusing Homogenization into Differentiation

Tops Creating Powerful Shared Visions

SHE: One thing became clear. As Tops hardened into their separate territories, they lost sight of the wholes – both their Top system as a whole and Dynamics Unlimited as a whole. There was no sense of their shared collective mission and vision. So during the weekend retreat – The Quest for Renewed Excellence – they began work on their shared vision, both for themselves and Dynamics Unlimited. *What are our fondest wishes for what this system is and will become?* The work on vision and mission is continuing. It's clear to Tops that the context they live in is full of complexities as well as issues for which there are no clear-cut yes or no answers. Conflicts are likely to arise, as you would expect if Tops were to work their way toward facing and resolving difficult issues. In the presence of conflict, it will be important for Tops to be able to come back and be grounded again in their powerful shared visions of the Top system and Dynamics Unlimited.

HE: An important contribution of homogenization. Even in the presence of our different responsibilities, being clear about the commonality that grounds us – our common vision, our shared mission.

Tops Walking in One Another's Shoes

SHE: Yes, and there's more. It also became clear that as Tops hardened into territoriality, they had little in-depth knowledge of one another's work other than the guarded information they shared. They explored several ways to remedy that. One of the more interesting – and challenging – was to find ways "to walk in one another's shoes," that is, to find ways of experiencing directly one another's worlds. This is having the effect of increasing each Top's connection with the whole. There is a second, immensely powerful, contribution that this strategy is making which I'll describe when we get to infusing integration into differentiation.

HE: Isn't there an additional bonus should one of these key players become incapacitated or leave? There's bench strength at the top.

Tops Sharing High Quality Information

SHE: Yes, and this "walking in one another's shoes" has generally led to a more open sharing of information. Tops are now being kept abreast of developments in one another's areas, of issues each is facing. It's clear that developments in one area are likely to have implications for other areas. Sharing, pooling, and analyzing information opens up new areas – new dangers and opportunities – that the whole system needs to be dealing with.

HE: It sounds like they've moved quite a distance from the situation you described where the "Mine" mentality was shaping what information was shared and what wasn't.

The Dynamics Unlimited Softball League

SHE: On a lighter note, yet one that will directly affect the whole organization, one Top suggested that, since our work has focused on the power of context, wouldn't it be interesting if we experienced one another in very different contexts? This has led to the creation of DU's Softball League. Among its rules: Each team must have one player who has absolutely no understanding of the game, and each team must have two players with an age difference of 20+ years.

HE: Hmm. Should the Tops be on the same team or different teams? Interesting implications.

SHE: I don't think you and I need to decide.

HE: I'm eager to learn about the *immensely powerful contribution* you mentioned earlier.

Infusing Integration into Individuation

SHE: When Tops were locked into territoriality, there was little to no productive integration in the sense of members working together, supporting one another in common purpose. Tops were basically operating in their separate individuated realms.

So we explored with them the possibilities of infusing the connectedness of integration into the separateness of individuation.

Tops become coaches to one another

SHE: As the Tops were discussing ways of using their meetings more productively, we suggested a process we've used successfully in other settings. In essence, Tops become coaches to one another. Top meetings become settings for mutual coaching, a structured process in which Tops take turns laying out where they are on the projects they're dealing with, what they're attempting to accomplish, and the issues they're facing. Then they get focused coaching from the other Tops. The purpose of the coaching is to move one another ahead.

HE: This is quite a shift. From being defensive and protective to becoming coaches to another.

SHE: From being defensive and protective to being committed to the *other's* success.

And notice what this shift accomplishes. Through mutual coaching, Tops gain a deep understanding of and *appreciation* for one another's worlds. They gain expert input from other Tops, they experience connectedness and mutual support, and they're strengthened in their own work while becoming committed to the success of other Tops.

HE: This feels like *both* integration and homogenization.

SHE: Zestful integration and zestful homogenization.

HE: How is this working out with DU's Tops?

SHE: Just think about it. Apart from its impact on individual Tops, through the process, new dangers the system is facing come to the surface, along with new opportunities the system could be exploring. And now the Top system as a whole is aware of these and more robustly focused on them.

HE: This sounds to me a lot like SHAPING.

SHE: That *is* the idea underlying all of this work. Illuminating context, and reversing these dances of blind reflex is the key to bringing THE PLAN to life.

Chapter 11: The Annotated Slide Show For Middles

A Tale of Middle Systems

Commentary: *This is a story of a potentially Robust Middle system, a system with outstanding capacity to deal with the challenges and opportunities it is facing.*

HE: I'm going to be interested in this because, frankly, I don't see Middles as a system. I see them as separate individuals going about their business, each with his and her own job to do.

SHE: That's how most people see Middles. But think about it this way. Water – liquid, ice, steam. One substance, three different states. When it comes to Middles, you are only seeing one state.

HE: And there are others?

SHE: Amazing others.

Here is how it begins

"We don't feel like a system"

Commentary: *Here is a fine collection of people, selected and promoted based on their abilities and performance track records. Each has his and her specific area of responsibility to lead, manage, supervise, coach, or otherwise service. They do not experience themselves as a system, yet they are one with great potential for contributing to the success of their organization.*

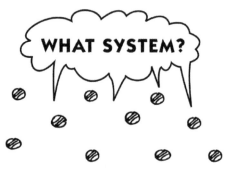

Here they are in a tearing context

Commentary: *Here they are in a tearing context, one that draws them away from one another and out toward the individuals and groups they are to lead, manage, supervise, or otherwise service.*

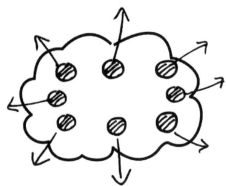

Middle system in a tearing context

The Middle system adapts

Commentary: *The Middle system adapts by individuating. Individual Middles move away from one another and out toward those individuals and groups they lead, manage, supervise, coach, or otherwise service.*

Individuation is an adaptive response to the tearing condition the system is facing, enabling individual Middles to service the individuals and groups they are designated to service. If they don't individuate, they don't do their jobs. Individuation is not the problem; what happens next is.

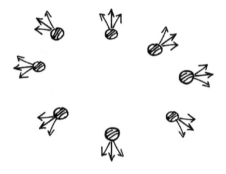

The Middle system individuating

Sclerosis sets in

Commentary: *Middles reflexively harden in their individuated state. Inertia sets in, with processes moving in the direction they are already moving. Middles become increasingly separate from one another, with their energies focused on the individuals and groups they service.*

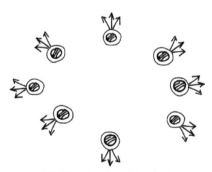

*Middles hardened in their
separateness*

HE: This looks a lot like Tops differentiating.

SHE: That's a common source of confusion. Let me try to clear it up.

          The Top and Middle systems are coping with distinctly different contexts.

          The members of the Top system are collectively accountable for the whole. Middles have no collective accountability, not in this state at least. They are accountable only for their job.

          The Top system as a whole is dealing with complexity and uncertainty.

          In response, the Top system differentiates and develops structures and processes for coping with that complexity and uncertainty.

          The Middle system is dealing with forces that are drawing each Middle out to his and her assignment.

          In the Top system story, it's the *functions* that harden into territories.

          In the Middle system story, it's *individual Middles* who harden in their isolation.

HE: I need to think about this.

Middle Isolation: Neither Power nor Love

Commentary: *The Middle system has fallen into a pattern of member isolation, in which individuation (separateness) predominates and all other processes (Integration, Differentiation, and Homogenization) are submerged.*

If a Robust system is a system of Power and Love, it is clear that the Middle system has neither Power nor Love.

Isolation: Neither Power nor Love

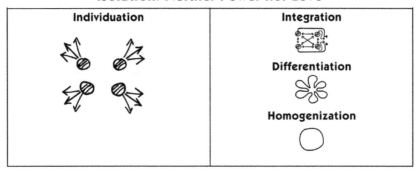

Individuation	Integration
	Differentiation
	Homogenization

Middles exist in their separate, isolated state

In the absence of integration, there is no functioning Middle whole, and there is no mission of the Middle system. The very notion of having a collective mission doesn't exist.

In the absence of a functioning whole with its own mission, there is no possibility of developing differentiated strategies for achieving such a mission.

HE: It's interesting that this systemic picture of the Middle system as one of neither Power nor Love fits with the common image of Middles as weak, individually *and* collectively.

SHE: It should come as no surprise since the one causes the other. You're simply seeing where that weakness comes from.

AN IMPORTANT PIECE OF SYSTEMS KNOWLEDGE!!

The pattern systems fall into shapes the consciousness of system members

Commentary: *The pattern Middles have fallen into shapes their consciousness: how they experience themselves, others, their system, and other systems. And then they behave consistently with that consciousness.*

An "I" consciousness emerges

Commentary: *Members of the Middle system fall into an "I" consciousness, one which is a natural corollary of their separateness from one another, their individuated state.*
    Elements of the "I" consciousness:
- *Members feel **unique**, having little in common with one another.*
- *Members feel **competitive** with one another: Who am I better than? Worse than? Better off than? Worse off than?*
- *Members are **evaluative** of one another, often on surface issues. How emotional or rational others are: How they dress, their accent, skin color, religion.*
- *And members feel that there is **no collective power** among them.*

A vicious cycle develops

Commentary: *Being apart in this isolated, individuated state generates the "I" consciousness, and the "I" consciousness reinforces staying apart. Why would I connect with people with whom I have little in common, who I am competitive with, evaluative of, and so forth?*
    This cycle serves to solidify separateness, the isolation pattern, making it resistant to change.

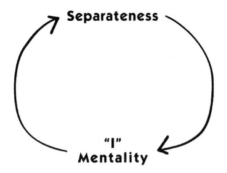

The consequences for individual Middles of this neither Power nor Love pattern

- **Weak.** *This isolated form weakens individual Middles.*
- **Unsupported.** *They experience the pressures of the system alone, unsupported, not part of Tops or Workers, and not connected with one another.*
- **Uninformed.** *Their system-wide information is thin.*
- **Negative feedback.** *Since they are often torn between the conflicting needs, demands, and priorities of others, it is easy to fall short for one party or another, or all parties.*
- **Incompetent.** *As a consequence, Middles may get regular messages regarding their inadequacy, and may come to believe that they are in fact incompetent.*

The consequences of this pattern for the system

Commentary: *The form the Middle system has fallen into also has system-wide consequences:*
- *There's a lack of coordination among system parts; coordination becomes one more complication Tops need to deal with.*
- *Middles are vulnerable to being blind-sided by other Middles. Actions taken unilaterally by one Middle have consequences for other Middles and their groups.*
- *Feelings of unfairness arise stemming from uncoordinated uneven actions (How come that group got computer upgrades... casual Fridays... paid Christmas party... exercise bikes... and we didn't?)*

- *There is lack of support for Tops (Tops' complaints: I can't get consistent information from them; I can't get my initiatives implemented consistently by them; I get too much dependency, not enough entrepreneurial action from them.)*

Needless to say, these weakened, uninformed, disconnected Middles are not functioning as the Integrating Mechanism of the system.

Without awareness or choice

Commentary: *The Middle system – with its capable, intelligent, well-intentioned members – has fallen out of the possibility of being a Robust system. It has fallen into a pattern of member isolation, a pattern of neither Love nor Power. Relationships among peers range from indifferent to conflictual. There are tensions among Middles, between Middles and those they lead, manage, and support, and between Middles and their Tops. Individual contributions often fall short, and, since there is no collective Middle system, there are no collective Middle contributions. This disintegrated condition can readily give the impression that this is not a system, more like a scattering of unconnected individuals. It is, however, a system, a regularly recurring one, one that has fallen blindly and reflexively into this dysfunctional neither Love nor Power form. And, in their system-blindness, Middles have no understanding of how their own behavior has brought all of this about.*

HE: I still think most people would find it hard to see a whole Middle *system.*

SHE: Unfortunately, that is how most Middles – and Tops too – feel. They feel there is no Middle system, just a collection of separate individuals. And once you believe that, that limits your possibilities for strengthening Middles individually and collectively, as well as the organization.

HE: But you know different?

SHE: I had a flash of insight a few years back. Then it seemed like a major breakthrough. Now it looks obvious.

HE: What do you mean?

SHE: Context. Putting it all in context.

That's more than a motto. Systems react to their contexts.

The Top system reacts to complexity by differentiating.

The Bottom system, as we will see, reacts to vulnerability by coalescing.

And the Middle system reacts to tearing by dispersing.

In each case, we're observing the system in its context-influenced state. So, this so-called "collection of separate individuals" is simply the Middle system in its dispersed state.

This understanding is critical because, once we recognize the Middle system as a system, both its weaknesses and possibilities are revealed.

Creating Middle Robust Systems

SHE: Once again, by looking at the chart, both the problem and the path toward solution become clear. There is no apparent system here, merely what appears to be that "collection of isolated individuals," stuck in their separateness.

As you look at this picture, what's the first thing you see this Middle system needing?

Isolation: Neither Power nor Love

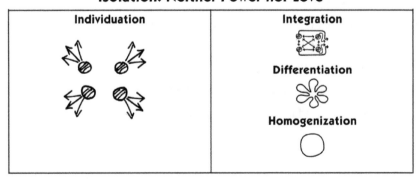

HE: There is no connection. So, integration is needed, a coming together, a connection, some interaction.

SHE: Exactly. Integration is the essential missing ingredient. Without integration there is no whole system to work with. And once a *semblance* of a system is created, Middles can then begin to explore how they strengthen one another individually and collectively. If this were a mechanical system, all of this would be obvious.

Systemic Awareness

HE: But we are not a mechanical system.

SHE: No, and so long as Middles at Dynamic Unlimited were in their "I" mentality, there was no possibility of creating a Robust Middle system. So, the goal of the presentation was to help Middles shift from a local perspective to a systemic one.

HE: Let me see if I now understand that shift.

They needed to recognize that what was happening to them was not specific to them, that it is a regularly recurring pattern in Middle systems.

SHE: Exactly.

HE: They needed to recognize that their experiences of one another were not reflections of reality, but that they were the *consequences* of this isolation pattern that they had fallen into.

SHE: Sounds good so far.

HE: And that if they changed the pattern, they would begin to experience one another quite differently.

SHE: That was our goal.

HE: That is a huge leap of faith we ask people to make.

SHE: It's not just faith. It's theory-based faith. That's different. It's a theory that can be tested.

HE: So how did it work?

SHE: As best as one could hope for. They said: *Let's give it a try.*

A Fundamental Shift in Perspective

From Personal	To Systemic
Specific. Our experiences as Middles feel like thay are specific to our particular collection of Middles and our particular circumstances.	**Patterns.** What we are experiencing is a pattern, one that occurs regularly in Middle systems.
Reality. How we experience ourselves and others feels like a reflection of who we and they *really* are.	How we experience ourselves and others is a consequence of this pattern of isolation we have fallen into. What we see is not all there is.
Change. Change comes by fixing, firing, rotating, replacing, retraining the people, ourselves and others.	Change the pattern and you will transform how Middles experience themselves.

Infusing Integration into Individuation

SHE: Individuation is what Middles *need* to do. It's their job, being out there leading, managing, supervising, coaching. Yet, when Middles are stuck in this isolated pattern, individuation is anemic.

HE: Anemic? How can you say that? These Middles might be giving it their all, doing their best to provide whatever service they're supposed to be providing. That's not necessarily anemic.

SHE: Anemic is judged not by effort but by what's possible. The experiment we were going to undertake with DU's Middles was to explore what new levels of individuation could be attained by infusing some robust Integration into the process.

Robust Integration: Middles as Intelligence Operatives

SHE: DU's Middles agreed to try a robust Integration process.

1. They agreed to meet regularly, and once a meeting schedule was set, they would stick to it despite all the conflicting demands on their attention. For a few geographically dispersed Middles, meetings were virtual. They also made arrangements for spontaneous check-ins if something needed immediate attention.

2. They would share information. The image they developed of themselves was that of an intelligence operation: in addition to doing their work, they were also gatherers of system intelligence.

3. They would use their pooled intelligence to diagnose system issues: What new developments are arising? Dangers to be dealt with? Opportunities to be seized?

4. They would manage system functioning by coordinating with one another, seeing that system parts move in sync with one another. Cut down on awkward surprises.

5. They would share best practices. Learning about successes in one Middle's domain might be beneficial in others.

6. They would function as mutual coaches to one another, helping one another move through whatever difficulties they were facing.

The goal was to develop a zestful dance between individuating and integrating – back and forth, individuating and integrating, individuating and integrating.

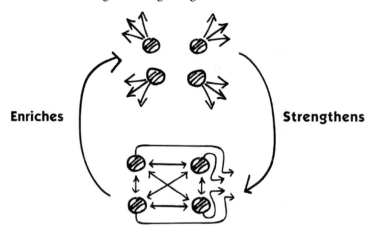

Enriches   **Strengthens**

HE: You were essentially creating a virtuous cycle.

SHE: How do you see that working?

HE: That robust Integration – sharing information, diagnosing system issues, sharing best practices – all of that strengthens Individuation, so when Middles move back out, they are more informed, better connected, they have a better sense of the whole system, and they may have better solutions to problems they face.

They are simply more secure and more capable of providing whatever services they should be providing.

SHE: That's moving from anemic to robust Individuation.

HE: Yes, and then, by sharing their enhanced experiences "out there" I would assume that the Integration meetings would also become richer with pooled intelligence.

SHE: From anemic to robust Integration.

HE: This is all great theory but how is this working out?

SHE: Middles are actually enjoying their new power. They feel part of a team. They feel supported, no longer facing the pressures of the system alone. There is still work to be done. They need to determine how to use their time together efficiently, better ways to make decisions and solve problems. They need to not let their newly developing strength and confidence lead them into becoming a cult – to find ways to keep other parts of the system informed.

HE: These *are* important issues, but they are issues the Middles are working on *together*. That's a long way from the isolation they had been experiencing.

The whole system is strengthened

SHE: Yes, and notice something else. Notice the *system-wide* function these Middles are serving. In addition to strengthening themselves and one another:

They are providing more informed leadership to the individuals and groups they serve *and* they are providing an important service to Tops.

With a strong Middle system, Tops are becoming more comfortable in putting more responsibility into that Middle system. It decreases the Tops' complexity, making more room for Tops to do SHAPING.

HE: I'm beginning to see how all this comes together.

SHE: This is what we understood when we suggested that Dynamics Unlimited stick with THE PLAN. We knew that it could work.

The secret to bringing THE PLAN into fruition lay in unleashing the robust system potential of Top, Middle, and Bottom systems.

Tops are better able to have their initiatives moved consistently down through the system, and they are more likely to get consistent information up from the Middles.

And Middles are able to provide more informed leadership to Workers.

HE: This sounds a lot like Middles are the INTEGRATING MECHANISM OF THE SYSTEM. They're providing information, resources, and support throughout the system, to one another and to all the individuals and groups they serve.

SHE: Doesn't it? That's great, and this is just the beginning of Middles' potential as a Robust System.

Creating a Robust Whole Middle System

HE: Just the beginning? I thought this was the goal: to develop the Middles into being the INTEGRATING MECHANISM OF THE SYSTEM. That's THE PLAN. What else is possible?

SHE: The Middle system has one potential that no other part of the system has.

HE: I'm listening.

SHE: One persistent lack of understanding regarding the Middle place is the notion that Middles have *no independent perspective* of their own. We saw that when we were dealing with individual Middles, and we see it again with Middle systems.

HE: Even those functioning as INTEGRATING MECHANISMS?

SHE: Even those. It's as if the *sole* business of the Middle system is to service *others*. This virtuous cycle you described is a much-improved way of doing just that.

HE: And didn't we just demonstrate how this Individuation/ Integration dance does that, and does it well?

SHE: Yes, and that's marvelous. And there is still another possibility for the Middle system.

HE: I'm eager to hear it.

SHE: Here's a question for you: Who has the best picture of the entire system?

HE: You would think Tops do.

SHE: Not really, given the complexity of their world. Talk to Tops and they'll tell you it's like being in a forest and all you see from their height is the tops of the trees.

         Think about it. A zestfully integrating/individuating Middle system has a whole-system perspective that no other part of the system has. The question is: what do they do with that?

HE: I'm not sure I understand.

A Mission of Our Own

SHE: Does this Middle system have a mission of its own, a mission that is separate from the individual missions of its members?

HE: Isn't being the INTEGRATING MECHANISM OF THE SYSTEM just such a mission? It's a mission of the Middle system that is separate from the individual missions of its members. What else is there?

SHE: Let's look again at the Middle No Love/No Power chart. What has our strategy been to this point?

HE: We've brought Integration into play. A virtuous cycle has been created whereby Individuation and Integration are now strengthening and enriching one another. Middles are becoming "masters of Individuation."

SHE   Right. So now we have a whole system that zestfully individuates and zestfully integrates. So, what's left?

HE: I'm not sure I understand.

SHE: Just look at the chart. What's missing?

HE: Homogenization and differentiation. And, actually, it looks like the integration process is also increasing homogenization, with more shared information and more mutual understanding.

SHE: Probably true. So now, what's left?

HE: Differentiation. But I don't see any place for it.

SHE: Why is that?

HE: Aha! I get it. For there to be differentiation, the Middle system would need to have some project of its own, something *it* wants to create. And then differentiation could come into play, new structures and processes for working that project. But the Middle system doesn't have such a project.

SHE: Precisely my point. But it *could* have such a project. Given its unique perspective, it could identify and undertake such projects stemming from its unique perspective.

HE: For example?

SHE: Well, here are some questions the Middles are asking:

- *What is missing in the system that we can make happen?*
- *What persistent problem exists that we could resolve?*
- *What can we do that has never been done before?*
- *What can we do better than it has been done before?*

HE: Interesting questions. Have they come up with answers?

SHE: Not as yet, but interesting possibilities are being explored.

HE: So once a project is settled on, that's when differentiation comes into play. *What strategies do we pursue in working this project?*

SHE: Exactly. That's when the Middle system expresses its full potential.

Zestfully individuating *and* zestfully integrating.

Zestfully differentiating *and* zestfully homogenizing.

A robust system of Power and Love.

HE: And how is this working out with DU's Middles? Wait, I think I know. A work in progress.

SHE: Exactly.

Chapter 12: The Annotated Slide Show For Workers

A Tale of Bottom Systems

The Bottom System's Dance of Blind Reflex

Commentary: *This is a story of a potentially Robust Bottom system, a system with outstanding capacity to deal with the challenges and opportunities it faces in its world of vulnerability.*

Here is how it begins

The front line

Commentary: *Here they are, the workers, the front line people, those who produce the organization's products and render its services. This is a friendly, energetic, talented, knowledgeable collection of individuals.*

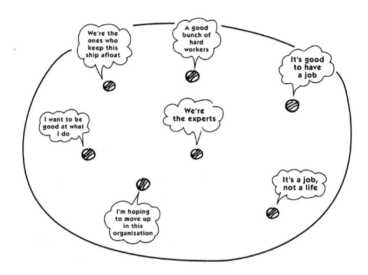

SHE: To this point we've been able to observe a whole organic system as it adapts to a context of accountability, complexity, and uncertainty by differentiating:

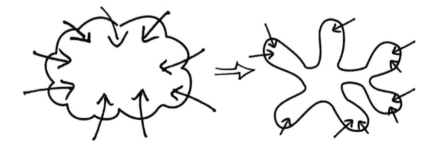

and how it adapts to a tearing context by individuating:

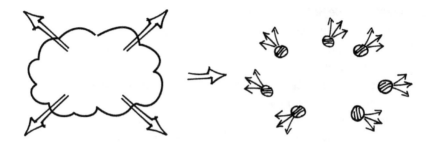

and now we're going to observe a whole organic system in a context of vulnerability:

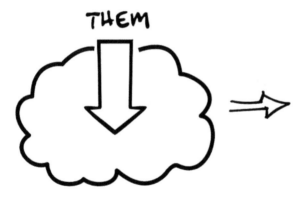

The Bottom system in a world of vulnerability

Commentary: *Here is the Bottom system engaging in a world of vulnerability – changes are coming at the systems that can affect workers' lives in major and minor ways, and that can jeopardize the very survival of the Bottom system. Jobs are being lost; there are demands for new skills, pressures to do more with less; contracts are being renegotiated with less favorable terms for members of the Bottom system; operations are being shut down or shipped to locations with less expensive labor costs. The Bottom system is in danger of being weakened or eliminated.*

The Bottom system adapts by coalescing

Commentary: *The Bottom system reacts by coalescing.*

Systemically, coalescing is homogenizing and integrating.

Differences among members diminish in importance while their commonality, their one-ness predominates.

And the Bottom system integrates, with members connecting with one another, sharing, and supporting one another in common cause.

As the Bottom system coalesces internally, it becomes disconnected from the rest of the system. Members experience themselves as different – differentiated – and separate – individuated – from the rest of the organization.

Coalescence is an adaptive response to threat. It provides the experience, if not the reality, of safety in the collective.

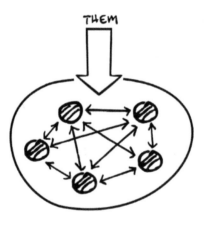

The Bottom system coalescing

Sclerosis sets in

Commentary: *Coalescence hardens, and the barrier that both binds the Workers together and separates them from the rest of the system thickens.*

Workers' bonds with one another deepen, and their experience of their difference from the others in the rest of the system, and their disconnectedness from them, also deepens.

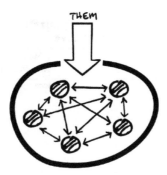

Coalescence hardens

Love internally, Power externally

Commentary: *The Bottom system has fallen out of the possibility of being a Robust system and into a pattern of Love internally (homogenized and integrated) and Power in relationship to the rest of the organization (differentiated and individuated):*

The Bottom System Internally
Love without Power

Dominant Love Processes	Submerged Power Processes
Homogenization	Differentiation
⬭	✿
Integration	Individuation

"We are One and connected with one another."

Relationship with the Organization
Power without Love

Dominant Power Processes	Submerged Love Processes
Differentiation	Homogenization
Individuation	Integration

"We are different and separate from THEM"

HE: I can see how the Bottom system becomes differentiated from the rest of the organization, but so long as Workers are in the organization, certainly some degree of integration is required simply to do their work.

SHE: You are right, and *minimal* integration is what develops, just enough to get the job done, and no more.

HE: Grudging integration.

SHE: Could be.

AN IMPORTANT PIECE OF SYSTEMS KNOWLEDGE!!

The pattern systems fall into shapes the consciousness of system members

Once Bottom systems fall into this internal Love and external Power pattern, that pattern shapes how Workers experience themselves and the rest of the system, and they then behave consistently with that consciousness.

A WE versus THEM consciousness emerges

Commentary: *Workers fall into a WE/THEM mentality that follows naturally from the pattern they've fallen into.*

Workers experience their difference from THEM, experiencing themselves as some variation of "good" (unjustly victimized, special, caring, warm, supportive, morally superior, right), while experiencing the others – THEM – as some variation of "bad" (greedy, insensitive, inept, uncaring, cold, distant).

The WE/THEM mentality shapes how Workers interact with the others – keeping separate, resisting the others, avoiding them, being sarcastically formal, poking fun at, sniping, ignoring, or sabotaging THEM.

HE: I guess this is what one could mean by *minimal* integration.

SHE: Negative connection.

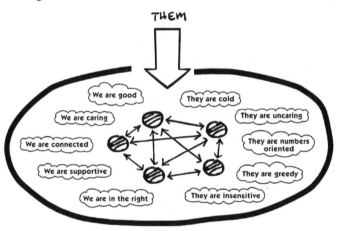

Bottom system members in their WE/THEM consciousness

A vicious cycle develops

The coalesced structure results in the "WE/THEM" mentality which then leads to actions that reinforce the coalesced structure, which reinforces the "WE/THEM" mentality, and on and on it goes.

The vicious cycle serves to solidify the Love internally and Power externally structure, making it resistant to change.

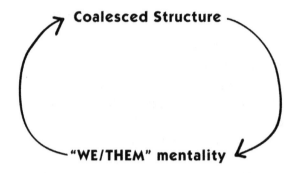

Coalesced Structure

"WE/THEM" mentality

Relationship issues among Workers unfold

Commentary: Relationships among members of the Bottom system begin to fray. The tensions that develop are the natural consequences of the Love without Power pattern they have fallen into.

- *Some members may be feeling overly constrained by the group, feeling the need for freedom. (Individuation is raising its head and is being suppressed.)*
- *There may be disagreements over the strategy and direction the group should be taking and these come up against pressures for uniformity. (Differentiation is raising its head and is being suppressed.)*
- *There are pressures to maintain the commonality and connectedness among group members. There are tensions between those reinforcing the WE (guardians of the WE) and those feeling constrained by it.*
- *Deviants are pressured, cajoled, threatened, or loved into line.*
- *When all else fails, dissidents are "exiled" from the group; they become "scabs," or are ignored, treated as invisible.*
- *Some dissidents self-censor, remain "closeted" in order to maintain their membership in the WE.*
- *Unilateral actions threaten the unity of the WE and are condemned in favor of consensual decision-making or non-contestable fiats from the Workers' leader. For some Workers such actions are stifling and spirit-crushing.*

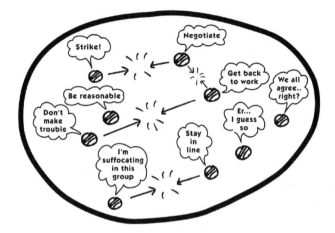

Tension within the Bottom system

Relationship issues between the Workers and the rest of the organization unfold

Commentary: *Relationship issues develop between the WE and THEM. Again, these are the natural consequences of the Power without Love pattern they have fallen into.*

Workers' relationships with higher-ups can range from indifferent, resistant, defensive, aggressive, to antagonistic and subversive. (Why wouldn't you act this way?)

Systemic issues unfold

Commentary: *The Bottom system is disengaged from the larger organization. For members, the organization is their Bottom system and not the larger organization.*

Without awareness or choice

Commentary: *All of this has unfolded without awareness or choice. A potentially Robust Bottom system has fallen into a dysfunctional pattern of Love without Power internally, and Power without Love in relation to the rest of the organization. The consequences: individual stress; broken, non-cooperative, conflictive relationships; diminished contributions; finger pointing and blame; and cluelessness, in the sense that none of the parties is aware of the part its blind reflexive behavior has played in bringing this about.*

SHE: The challenge for the Bottom system is to survive in its world of vulnerability, to become masters of vulnerability.

HE: But you know as well as I do that that's just not possible.

SHE: And why is that?

HE: Look, no matter what Workers do, they *are* vulnerable. They could be committed to the mission of the organization, learning new skills, adapting to changing circumstances, doing all the right things. And then, management shuts the operation down. Then where does that leave these masters of vulnerability?

SHE: Well prepared, I hope.

HE: Please elaborate.

SHE: You are right, of course. Times are particularly precarious for many Bottom systems. Globalization has disrupted many of the old power-equalizing tools: threats, slowdowns, strikes, hard bargaining. If all of that is too painful to management, they'll just take their operation someplace else.

HE: So, you agree with me?

SHE: No. It simply means Bottom systems need to develop more robust survival strategies – strategies for surviving *within* the organization *and* surviving *without* it. And neither is possible so long as Bottom systems are stuck in that sclerotic coalesced pattern in which they have both walled themselves in while walling the rest of the organization out.

Creating Robust Bottom Systems

SHE: Again, simply looking at the pattern reveals both the problem and the way ahead. This was their pattern for coping with vulnerability. What does it tell you?

The Bottom System Internally
Love without Power

Dominant Love Processes	Submerged Power Processes
Homogenization	Differentiation
Integration	Individuation

HE: They were coping with vulnerability by homogenizing and integrating: unity and togetherness.

SHE: Unity and togetherness.

HE: Those *are* virtues, aren't they?

SHE: They are, but pay attention to the costs.

Individuation is suppressed: individual freedom, brain power, and initiative are constrained.

Differentiation is suppressed: the possibility of exploring diverse survival strategies is limited.

But when you're locked in that WE consciousness, the mentality is: "In unity there is strength." Individuation and differentiation are experienced as threatening the strength of the WE.

HE: But those threats feel so real.

SHE: Yes, and that is the *illusion* of this Bottom context.

HE: It's a paradox. The adaptive survival pattern you have fallen into turns out to work against your survival.

SHE: Exactly, and to change that requires that huge leap of faith we've talked about.

HE: That theory-based leap of faith.

SHE: To understand that *what we see is not all there is.*

HE: You do seem energized about this.

SHE: This is *the* fundamental breakthrough. Without it, the rest is just words. Nothing will matter. Nothing will change.

HE: Change the pattern and a very different reality appears. That's the *big* message.

SHE: Yes, and we need to directly *experience* the shift before we can really believe it.

HE: Isn't this what is happening with the Tops? As they're working on homogenizing and integrating, they're beginning to experience one another quite differently.

SHE: A shift from defensive and protective territorialism to experiencing possibilities in one another. An immensely productive shift.

HE: And similarly with the Middles. As they're beginning to integrate regularly, they begin to experience one another quite differently.

SHE: A shift from that isolated "I" mentality to creative and productive partnership.

HE: And so how is this working out with Workers?

A Fundamental Shift in Perspective

From Personal	To Systemic
Specific. Our experiences as Workers, both of ourselves and the Tops and Middles feel specific to these particular people and our particular circumstances.	**Patterns.** What we are experiencing is a pattern, one that occurs regularly in Bottom systems.
Reality. How we experience ourselves and others feels like a reflection of who we and they *really* are.	How we experience ourselves and others is a consequence of the patterns we have fallen into: Love internally, Power in relation to the rest of organization
Change. Change comes by fixing, firing, rotating, avoiding, controlling, replacing, retraining the people, ourselves and others.	Change the pattern and you will transform how Workers experience themselves and Top and Middles.

SHE: The discussion was rich…eventually. There was some initial hesitation to speak at all.

HE: A reluctance to upset the unity?

SHE: Exactly. But then connections were made. Some talked about how they've felt oppressed, crushed, stifled by this unity. For some, the feelings were so strong they wanted to leave the group. Others owned up to the comfort this WE-ness provided.

HE: Comfort?

SHE: Like a security blanket. You can hide in the WE. No need to risk, or make yourself vulnerable. Just go along with the group.

HE: So, you're both comfortable and constrained.

SHE: That is the tension.

HE: Still, I'm sure people didn't want to give up the strength that comes with their unity. Where are they without that?

Unleashing Individuation and Differentiation

SHE: First, we need to accept that this so-called unity is *anemic*.

HE: Anemic?

SHE: It's built on the suppression of all that human potential in the Bottom system. The challenge is not to weaken that unity – though that's the fear – but to strengthen it.

How do we *increase* our strength by unleashing the submerged powers of individuation and differentiation?

How do we zestfully individuate *and* zestfully integrate? How do we tap into the rich diversity of knowledge, expertise, and experience that exists hidden in this Bottom system?

How do we create the safety and support that encourages – prods – members to come out from under the comforting blanket of the WE and bring to bear whatever unique capabilities they have?

HE: Once again, you're creating that virtuous cycle in which individuation and integration strengthen and enrich one another.

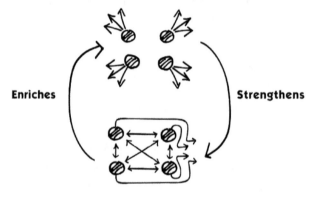

Enriches   **Strengthens**

SHE: Exactly. Once these fundamental processes are understood, it becomes clear that:

- integration by itself suppresses energy and weakens the system

- individuation is not a threat to integration – it's what supports and strengthens it

- robustness comes from zestfully expressing both.

HE: So how are they putting this into practice?

SHE: They've been compiling an inventory of their collective resources: the skills, expertise, and experience that each of them has. It's amazing what people are learning about one another.

And members are making commitments regarding actions they're willing to take, actions aimed at strengthening one another or the Bottom system as a whole.

HE: It will be interesting to see what develops out of that resources inventory. But, isn't there another missing piece to creating this robust Bottom system?

SHE: What's missing?

HE: Differentiation.

SHE: Okay, let's explore that.

When the Bottom system is stuck in its coalesced pattern and in the grips of the WE/THEM mentality, differentiation is experienced as threatening the unity of the WE. Endless hours of debate are spent arguing over *the* correct strategy to pursue. *Do we keep our heads down or do we challenge the system?* This is another myth that is experienced as an unshakeable truth: that there is the *one correct approach* and, if there are disagreements, we must debate until we all agree to pursue the one correct approach.

HE: Another case where the adaptive pattern you've fallen into ends up weakening your chances for survival.

SHE: Exactly. *The pattern one has fallen into shapes one's experience.* The big insight into systems life. Once it was understood, people began to explore multiple strategies, sometimes apparently conflicting ones, so long as all were grounded in a common mission: mastering vulnerability, surviving in a world of vulnerability.

The one-ness of homogenization

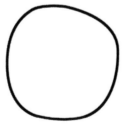

needed to be infused with the richness of differentiation:

What are the strategies we can pursue to reduce our vulnerability? We don't have to argue about which to pursue. None of us needs to be entrenched in any one strategy. The goal is to develop a differentiated Bottom system.

HE: What form is this taking?

SHE: One strategy is to make ourselves valuable: to pour our creative energies into the work of the system. To make ourselves so critical to the success of the system that we are indispensable.

HE: Becoming the system's PRODUCERS.

SHE: Yes, yet another strategy might be to stand firm for creating an equitable strategy with management. In return for our full support, these are the conditions we consider fair and reasonable.

HE: Tough and tender.

SHE: Tough, tender, *and political*. If you feel the political and economic system is rigged against you, get political! Get involved in changing systems you feel are unfair and oppressive. These are not either/or strategies. Any system member might be an active participant in *all* strategies. It's the *system* that elaborates its survival strategies by mastering differentiation.

HE: So, even as the system is differentiating, any member of the system might also be differentiating. Person as system. Interesting.

SHE: Important insight.

HE: So, with these differentiated strategies, the Bottom system is moving beyond PRODUCING.

SHE: As one member said, *No one said that's* all *we are. We PRODUCE, we PROTECT, and we TRANSFORM.*

HE: I feel a lot of power there.

SHE: *And* Love. Homogenization and Integration provide the commonality and connectedness that support all this power.

Partnering with THEM

SHE: There's more. The Bottom system might simultaneously pursue a strategy of developing more collegiality with management.

HE: Really?

SHE: Really. We're exploring all possibilities for mastering vulnerability.

HE: OK.

SHE: When we are stuck in our WE/THEM mentality, we experience ourselves as foreign to them and them to us. It's a relationship of Power without Love. We are different. We're some variation of good – victims, morally superior, democratic, humanistic – and they are some variation of bad – aloof, indifferent, mechanical, greedy. How much of this is real and how much the illusion of the WE/THEM mentality?

HE: Enter the act of theory-based faith.

Relationship with the Organization
Power without Love

Dominant Power Processes	Submerged Love Processes
Differentiation	Homogenization
Individuation	Integration

SHE: Exactly. We can't really know until we change the pattern. What if we explore the possibility of infusing homogenization into our relationships with them – our commonalities? What if we just begin to notice our WE/THEM mentality in operation, our evaluations of THEM – the names we use to describe them, the characteristics we attribute to them. What if we question the basis on which these evaluations are made?

Let's see what changes if we reach out and connect to one another – inside the organization through meetings and day-to-day contact, and outside through community service, participation in sports, etc.

HE: This could be dangerous. No matter what, we and they have different agendas. Wouldn't it be foolhardy to ignore that?

SHE: It would. All we are attempting in this *one* survival strategy is to establish, in our eyes and theirs, our commonality. The reality is: Yes, we are different *and* we are similar. We are differentiated *and* homogenized. It's harder to harm people with whom you share common humanity. Not impossible, but more difficult.

This is all about *zestful differentiation,* multiple strategies. That's the point. Not to settle on *the one,* nor to dismiss any prematurely.

Survival Without the Organization

HE: OK. I can see all of this. Multiple strategies. Release the talents of system members, pursue multiple survival strategies, build connections with the rest of the organization. And then they shut the plant down.

SHE: And that may require the fundamental shift that underlies all the rest. If the plant closes, that simply demonstrates what was always true. *You are alone.* Membership in the organization gave you the illusion and false comfort that you were not.

It's a mistake to wait until the plant closes to work on survival without the organization. That should be your agenda from the start. Education. Staying abreast of new technologies. Building your network. Developing your portfolio of entrepreneurial possibilities. Using your experience in the organization for all it can teach you about life without the organization.

HE: Given all of that, is it possible for Workers to still function as system PRODUCERS?

SHE: Yes, but when we ask them they say *"We're PRODUCERS, but understand: that's not all we are."*

HE: I get it.

Coda: Take One

HE: Well, things do seem to be humming along at Dynamics Unlimited. Lots of creative energy.

SHE: It's not bad.

HE: Seems to be widespread commitment to THE PLAN.

SHE: Seems to be.

HE: So now, what I wonder is: Will it last?

SHE: That's a good question.

HE: Come on. You know that usually means you don't know, or you need time to think.

SHE: It's both. Just consider what we've opened up here.

HE: You did what you set out to do. You created awareness. You turned the lights on at Dynamics Unlimited. You took them all – Tops, Middles, Workers, and even some of the Customers – from context-blindness to context-sight.

SHE: Yes, but your question is: *Will it last?* Think about what this means. Life will go on and, as it does, it will bring its unanticipated events.

         Tops will be confronted with new complexities and difficult decisions to make.

         Workers will run up against new problems that Tops and Middles have created and should be fixing.

         Middles are going to find themselves caught between conflicting demands, agendas, and priorities of others.

And Customers are going to come up against painful snags in delivery.

HE: Stuff happens.

SHE: Yes it does. Stuff happens, and it happens, and it keeps on happening. Unrelentingly. So, then your question *"will it last?"* depends on continuing awareness and choice in the face of stuff after stuff after stuff. And that's tough to maintain.

HE: You would think it would get easier over time.

SHE: You would think so.

HE: You're still hesitant.

SHE: Just being realistic. We can't trivialize what we've opened up for people.

Awareness is an important step, but it is a first step, because then we are faced with choice. With awareness comes the end of innocence. It's clear you could go this way or that. But those can be hugely different directions, demanding hugely different parts of ourselves.

For example, in my Bottom context, facing some incredibly inept action THEY have taken, every bone in my body pulls me toward whining and complaining, to feeling like the suffering victim of *their* actions. The pull is powerful. But now, with this damn gift of awareness, I can't hide from this other choice. *Stop holding THEM responsible! Must I?* So now I think, come on, get busy finding ways you – with your skills, your network, your energy – can fix this mess they've created. And then I think: *Why must I?*

HE: I understand. It's more than simply choosing this way of that. It's like the path you go down determines the *person* you will be.

SHE: That's a powerful way of putting it. But, in the moment it is easy to lose sight of that possibility. Or, even if you see it, to say *No thanks, I think I'll just stay the person I am.*

HE: You don't seem optimistic.

SHE: I'm just being realistic. Awareness creates this tension. Every bone in my body is pulling me.

In the Customer context, the pull of righteousness is intense. *For goodness sake, I am entitled! Why should I let that go?*

In the Top context, the pull of responsibility is intense. *I'm Top, it's my responsibility! How do I let that go?*

In the Middle Context, the pull to slide into the middle, to fix, to solve is intense. *They need me! How do I let that go?*

HE: So, will it last?

SHE: That's still an open question. So much depends on the ability of individuals, moment by moment, event after event, to be aware, and, in those moments of awareness, to have the courage to make the right choices.

HE: That's the best you can offer after all this work?

SHE: Sorry, that's it.

HE: I'm really surprised. And, frankly, disappointed. Given what I've been seeing at DU, I would have expected a much more up-beat picture from you.

SHE: And what have you've been seeing that gives you such optimism?

HE: *Systems. Robust human systems. Top, Middle, Bottom.*

SHE: So systems will make the difference?

HE: I do believe they will.

SHE: And so you disagree with me?

HE: I do.

SHE: Good!

HE: Good?

SHE: From the moment I saw you doing crossword puzzles in the waiting room I knew you were right for Microscope.

HE: What? Has this been some kind of test of me?

SHE: Sort of. So now let's end this. A new ending.

       Take Two.

Coda: Take Two

HE: Well, things do seem to be humming along at Dynamics Unlimited. Lots of creative energy.

SHE: It's not bad.

HE: Seems to be widespread commitment to THE PLAN.

SHE: Seems to be.

HE: So now, my question is: Will it last?

SHE: Oh, I feel sure that it will.

HE: You seem confident.

SHE: I'm very confident.

HE: Wow! What gives you such confidence? Is it that people seem to be living from their stands? Saying NO to the reflex dances?

SHE: That's very gratifying, but that alone won't do it.

HE: What then?

SHE: It's the systems.

HE: Please elaborate.

SHE: I told you at the outset that you cannot change systems one person at a time. One thousand enlightened employees will not create an enlightened system.

HE: So, what are you seeing that gives you confidence?

SHE: I'm seeing the development of three Powerful Robust Systems at Dynamics Unlimited – at the Top, in the Middle, and on the Bottom.

I'm seeing zestful, individuating, people in each system using their unique experiences and talents to master the context-challenges their system is facing.

I'm seeing zestful, integrating people in each system working together, in various configurations, encouraging, challenging and supporting one another in common ventures.

I'm seeing zestful differentiating: each system developing an ever-changing variety of strategies for mastering the challenges that system is facing.

And I'm seeing zestful homogenizing: powerful shared values, experience, and talents permeating each system.

HE: That's terrific, but what gives you confidence that this will last?

What's to prevent Tops from falling back into territoriality and the "Mine" mentality? Or the Middles back into their separateness and the isolated "I" mentality? Or the Workers falling into "WE/THEM?" What about the power of the Dance of Blind Reflex? What stops that?

SHE: Immediate collective benefits.

HE: Huh?

SHE: As these three systems have formed, people have already experienced immediate benefits, results that have strengthened members and their Top, Middle, and Bottom systems.

For example, there is new excitement in the Bottom system as members feel freed up from the stifling conformity pressures they had been experiencing. There's new excitement and confidence as members work together, pursuing multiple and diverse strategies for coping with their vulnerability.

And in the Middle system, there is the immediate strengthening of members. Members no longer feeling alone, they're connected, part of a team, supported, having greater system-wide knowledge, and being better positioned to support Tops and Workers.

And in the Top system, members are enjoying and benefiting from the shift from protectiveness to openness and collaboration with one another. Their "territories" are being strengthened by the sharing of information and expertise, and by the mutual coaching they are engaging in. Members feel more confident in their system's ability to master the complexities the system is facing and will be facing.

HE: I see the potential for each system to get into a virtuous cycle.

SHE: Exactly, their robust forms produce positive results which then sustain and strengthen the system which continues to generate positive results and on and on it goes.

Each system has become a welcoming place, a space of partnership where members are both supported and challenged by one another.

HE: What else gives you confidence?

SHE: THE PLAN. Where it all began.

THE PLAN was not a possibility so long as each system and its members were in the grips of the Dance.

HE: Another good idea, doomed to failure.

SHE: Exactly. But Robust Systems have the capacity for implementing THE PLAN. THE PLAN gives each system a clear and lasting mission. *This is what we are about. This is what we do. This is the unique contribution we make to the survival and development of Dynamics Unlimited.*

So even as members leave the system and new members arrive, the orientation of new members is shaped by THE PLAN. *You have your job, your assignment, your area of responsibility, but collectively*

Our responsibility as Tops is to function as system Shapers.

Our responsibility as Workers is to function as system Producers.

Our job as Middles is to function as the Integrating Mechanism of the system,

And those folks, our Customers and potential Customers, they are our Validators.

HE: And that capacity comes from mastering the contexts they all are in.

SHE: Context, context, context.

The Costs of Whole System Context Blindness

Organizational System	Context	Danger	Adaptive Response	Sclerotic Predominant Processes	Sclerotic Submerged Processes	Dysfunctional Pattern	Organizational Issue
TOP	Complexity Uncertainty Accountability	Overwhelmed by Complexity	Differentiation	Differentiated Individuated	Homogenization Integration	Power Without Love	Territoriality
MIDDLES	Tearing	Torn Disintegrated	Individuation	Individuated	Integration Homogenization Differentiation	Neither Power Nor Love	Disintegration
BOTTOM	Vulnerability	Controlled Crushed Eliminated	Homogenization Integration	Internally Homogenized Integrated Externally Differentiated Individuated	Individuation Differentiation	Love without Power internally Power without Love externally	Disengagement

Afterword

A Personal Story of Discovery

I often work while listening to classical music courtesy of YouTube. One morning, as Mozart's magnificent Symphony #40 was playing, I happened to scroll through the comments and came across the following:

> *"Mozart is the greatest composer of all. Beethoven created his music, but the music of Mozart is of such purity and beauty that one feels he merely found it – that it has always existed as part of the inner beauty of the universe waiting to be revealed."*
>
> Albert Einstein

This reflects how I feel about the human systems theory underlying this book and my other work. I didn't create it, I found it, as if it has always existed as part of the inner beauty of the universe. Roseanne Cash has said something similar about the songs she has written: it's as if they're out there in the ether, and she had better go out and grab them before someone else did.

My research laboratories

I did not set out to be a theoretician of system life. In my early career, I was basically a designer, a creator of learning experiences. The niche that I carved out for myself dealt with learning in the context of total systems – organizations and communities. It was as a participant in and observer of these many organizational and community experiences that a framework for understanding systems – the wholes and the parts – began to emerge and then evolve over the years.

Two programs in particular have been central to my learning about human systems – the Power Lab and the Organization Workshop. Both have been created as settings in which participants can deepen their understanding of themselves in the context of social system life. At the same time, they have been rich learning opportunities for me to deepen my understanding of systems. Central to both programs are whole-system experiences.

In the Power Lab, participants are "born" into *The Society of New Hope*, a total immersion, three-class, social system with sharp differences in wealth and power. At the top are the Elite who own or control the bulk of the society's resources, including its money, housing, food, court, and work opportunities. At the bottom are the Immigrants who enter the society with little more than the clothes on their backs. And between the two are the Middles who manage the institutions of the Elite.

In the Organization Workshop, participants are "born" into a system in which there is an organization – composed of Tops, Middles, and Bottom groups - that interacts with Customers and potential Customers.

What made both the Power Lab and the Organization Workshop particularly rich laboratories for my learning about systems is that these are not role-play situations, that is, no one is instructed how to react. Conditions are created, people are placed into these conditions, and events unfold. This gave me opportunity after opportunity to observe *naturally* unfolding events. Still there remained the question: what was I seeing? And what to make of it all? My framework for seeing whole systems has evolved over many years, yet I do remember one powerful moment – a literal "awakening" in the middle of the night, startling my wife by blurting out "It's alive!" In that moment, I experienced the organic nature of the whole, the sense that the society was an entity in itself, a whole living *thing* with processes of the whole. Early on we would describe the whole as having cells and membranes, and boundaries that were impermeable (unhealthy), totally permeable (also unhealthy), and flexibly semi-permeable (some possibilities there). Yet I still had no language for the whole: what it is, what it does.

Patterns of relationships. Early on I found a welcoming, comforting, and inspiring conceptual home in the work of Ervin Laszlo, particularly his *The Systems View of the World*. Here is Laszlo describing systems as patterns of relationship, a concept that would eventually be fundamental to my work.

> *"Individuals come and go; [the systems] remain. It is not that [the systems] are immune to change themselves, but they do not change with the changes in membership... In each case there are*

146

> *sets of relationships which are conserved, even though all
> participants get themselves replaced sooner or later.[2]"*

It would be several years before I would be able to identify and name the consistent patterns of systemic relationship that characterized the organizational systems I had been working with, and likely *all* organizational systems: Top/Bottom, End/Middle/End, and Provider/Customer. It became clear how universal these systemic relationships were. *They were always there.* In our system lives, we regularly move in and out of these systemic relationships, sometimes on one side and sometimes on the other. In certain interactions we are Top with designated responsibility for some process, and in others we are Bottom as members in Top's process; in other interactions we are one of two or more Ends competing for a Middle's attention, and at other times we are Middle between two or more Ends; in still other interactions we are Provider of product or service to a Customer, and in other interactions we are the Customer.

The Dance of Blind Reflex: Part One. Although we are constantly moving in and out of these relationships, we are blind to them. We see the *people* we are interacting with, but we do not see the systemic relationships we are in. We came to notice, in that blindness, the regularly recurring reflexive dances of responsibility – from Bottom to Top, from Ends to Middle, from Customer to Provider, and the consequences those dances had for individuals, their relationships, their effectiveness and system contribution.

These three patterns of relationship and their responsibility dances account for much of the consistency in system interaction across the widest range of system types, *even though all participants get themselves replaced sooner or later.[3]*

Patterns of Process. The Power Lab offered a unique opportunity to study three different whole systems (Top/Elite, Middle/Managers, and Bottom/Immigrants) within the larger system of the community (the Society of New Hope). Once again, although each program had a fresh cast of characters – none of whom were instructed how to play their parts – the scenarios and themes played out by each system were remarkably consistent from Power Lab to Power Lab. In brief, Tops regularly had difficult relationships with one another, protecting their individual turfs, sending conflicting messages throughout the community, struggling with one another

---

[2] Laszlo (1972) p. 7.
[3] Oshry (2007). These systemic relationships are detailed in chapters 19-35.

over the culture, purpose and direction of the community. Those in the Bottom context quickly coalesced and would eventually have difficulty in maintaining that unity in the face of conflicting pressures. And Middles regularly became non-groups, with individuals Middles turned away from one another, focused on their respective responsibilities and their connections with *their* Top, and with little to no connection with one another.[4]

These were gross observations; what we lacked was a language of whole systems. Why were these Top, Middle, and Bottom systems developing so differently from one another? There were no systematic differences in the personal makeup of members from one system to the other, so the differences in subsequent system life could not be attributed to the characteristics of its members. Again from Laszlo:

> *Hence, to all intents and purposes, the characteristics of complex wholes remain irreducible to the characteristics of the parts... (N)ot only could we not compute the behavior of the whole from the behavior of the parts, but we would have to revise our computations with every change in "personnel." A hopeless as well as futile endeavor indeed.*[5]

What we were observing in the Power Lab were initially identical whole systems – that is, systems with no systematic differences in member makeup, interacting with three different environments. And the different scenarios that developed resulted from the processes each system employed in attempting to cope with the conditions of *its* immediate environment. The work then was to discover what were these processes of the whole.

Individuation and Integration. Middle and Bottom were the clearest and most dramatically different systems. In interacting with a diffusing environment, Middle systems members individuated, going about their separate businesses with members functioning as separate independent *wholes;* Bottom systems members integrated, coming together, functioning as *parts* of a single whole. Individuation and Integration. Part and whole. Separate and together. Independence and connectedness. These are universal whole-system processes. *They have always been there.*

Laszlo described the phenomenon of entities being independent wholes and component parts in systems from the sub-organic (sub-atomic) to the organic (human) to the supra-organic (groups and societies).[6]

---

[4] Oshry (1999). See particularly chapter 6.

[5] Laszlo (1972) p.8

[6] Laszlo (1972) pp.29-33

Arthur Koestler coined his own term for this phenomenon of whole and part as it related to the human being.

No man is an island – he is a holon. A Janus-faced entity who, looking inward, sees himself as a self-contained unique whole, looking outward as a dependent part.

And then there is Lewis Thomas' lyrical description of whole and part, individuation and integration, as they play out in the life cycle of slime mold cells.

At first they are single amebocytes swimming around, eating bacteria, aloof from each other, untouching, voting straight Republican. Then, a bell sounds, and acrasin is released by special cells toward which the others converge in stellate ranks, touch, fuse together, and construct the slug, solid as a trout. A splendid stalk is raised, with a fruiting body on top, and out of this comes the next generation of amebocytes, ready to swim across the same moist ground, solitary and ambitious.[7]

What was unique to our organizational systems was that there was no slime mold cell natural back and forth flow of individuation and integration. On the contrary, the tendency was to get stuck on one process or the other to the eventual detriment of system members, their relationships with one another, and their system.

Differentiation and homogenization. The unique Top story gave us insight into another pair of system processes. The Top system was entering an environment of shared accountability for the larger system. It was also a complex environment that the Top system was entering, with multiple difficult and unpredictable issues to deal with, and it was an environment with critical uncertainties regarding how best to shape and direct the system as a whole. Top systems regularly differentiated in response to these conditions. What was happening in the Top system was in sharp contrast to developments in the Bottom system. Whereas members of the Top system are becoming more specialized, more different from one another, in the Bottom, member differences are submerged and commonality predominates. *As the Top system is differentiating, the Bottom system is homogenizing.*

The interplay between differentiation and homogenization again appears to be a universal system phenomenon. For example, it fascinated me to see how organic systems develop survival strategies based on the balance of these

---

[7] Thomas (1974) pp.14-15

two processes, for example, contrasting the survival strategy of the human organism as a whole system with that of a common flatworm. The flatworm's survival strategy is based on limiting differentiation and emphasizing homogenization. The result: the flatworm doesn't do much by the standards of the human organism, but whatever capacity it does have is spread throughout the system. Cut off its head, and other parts of the flatworm have the capacity to generate a form of new head. The human organism's survival strategy is quite the reverse: maximizing differentiation at the cost of homogenization with the result that we have a much more varied capacity for engaging with our environments, but our lost parts are not so naturally replaceable. Although, given our amazingly differentiated brain, we are getting better at it.

The Dance of Blind Reflex: Part Two. Understanding these processes enabled us to unravel the mystery of how these three initially identical systems developed such uniquely different lives. Without awareness or choice, each system was blindly and reflexively adapting to its immediate environmental context. And difficulties developed within each system, as initially adaptive responses hardened into dysfunctional patterns.

The two faces of consciousness. There is a puzzle: Why do organic systems – the slime mold cell, the earthworm, the human organism – find successful balances of individuation and integration, differentiation and homogenization, while the supra-organisms of organizations, political groups, institutions, ethnic groups, and such are prone to imbalances resulting in painful and costly dysfunction? Why don't these supra-organic systems naturally find healthy, non-destructive, system-sustaining balances?

I suggest, and I leave it to future generations of researchers to investigate, that consciousness lies at the heart of that puzzle. Laszlo makes a useful distinction between subjectivity and consciousness. All organic systems possess subjectivity: they *react* to stimuli. Poke, heat or freeze flatworms, slugs, and the human body and they will react, but the capacity we humans have, thanks to our highly and fortuitously evolved cerebral cortex, is to think about our reactions. We can witness our reactions, and we can choose.

Organisms endowed with consciousness are liberated from the world of here and now experiences and can enter a quasi-autonomous world of their own creation…. Mere subjectivity is bound to the immediacy of events; only consciousness can liberate one from his actual experience and enable him to control it by his own will.[8]

---

[8] Laszlo (1972) pp. 91-95

This capacity to experience and then reflect on our experience and then make choices based on those reflections would appear to be an unvarnished human advantage. It is an advantage, but unvarnished it is not. On the positive side, as we have seen throughout this work, consciousness allows us to recognize dysfunction, understand it, and choose to remedy it. But consciousness is often what gets us in trouble in the first place. Our "special" advantage enables us to evaluate processes, to concoct myths and theories and value systems that elevate certain processes over others. Individuation is good and integration is bad, or the reverse. And once our myths and theories are established we are free to choose, to move straight ahead into self and system dysfunction. If Lewis Thomas' slime mold cells had our human consciousness, some of those individuating amebocytes might well choose to remain out in the world foraging alone rather than return and become part of that "socialist" slug. Fortunately for them, amebocytes are incapable of making such choices, but we, with our double-edged gift of consciousness can.

Power and Love. It was only as a result of my conversations with Adam Kahane and his work on Power and Love[9], that I asked: Are there system parallels to Power and Love? How do whole organic systems express their Power and Love? This led me to see the four whole-system processes in a new configuration: individuation and differentiation together being the whole-system equivalent of Power, the yang of system life, the unleashing of individual and group energy; and integration and homogenization together being the whole system equivalent of Love, the yin of system life, the oneness of members coming together and uniting in common purpose. Through that lens it also became clear that the processes of Power and Love support one another, and that blindly falling into – or unwisely choosing – one without the other leads to inevitable personal and whole-system destructive consequences. And it also became clear that if we were able see, understand, and master these whole-system processes, it would be possible for us to create sane, healthy, and productive systems – Robust systems, systems of Power and Love.

That still remains the goal.

Barry Oshry
Boston, September 2017

---

[9] Kahane (2010)

References

Adam Kahane. *Power and Love: A Theory and Practice of Social Change.* Berrett-Koehler, 2010

Adam Kahane. *Solving Tough Problems: An Open Way of Talking, Listening, and Creating New Realities.* Berrett-Koehler, 2004

Arthur Koestler. *The Ghost in the Machine.* Hutchinson, 1967

Ervin Laszlo. *The Systems View of the World.* George Braziller, 1972, Hampton Press, 1996

Lewis Thomas. *The Lives of a Cell.* Viking, 1974

Additional Resources

For more on the Power Lab, see:
Barry Oshry. *Leading Systems: Lessons from the Power Lab.* Berrett-Koehler, 1999

For more on the Organization Workshop, see:
Barry Oshry. *Seeing Systems: Unlocking the Mysteries of Organizational Life (2nd edition).* Berrett-Koehler, 2007

Additional information on both of these programs can be found at: www.powerandsystems.com.

For further reading on this organic systems perspective, see:
Barry Oshry. *The Systems Letter.* Microscope, 2017
Barry Oshry. *In the Middle.* Power+Systems, 1994
Barry Oshry. *The Possibilities of Organization.* Power+Systems, 1992
Barry Oshry. *The Organic Systems Perspective: A New Paradigm for Understanding and Intervening in Organizational Life,* Power+Systems, 2012
Barry Oshry. Transforming System Blindness into System Sight. https://www.youtube.com/watch?v=VYpO-pK7IFA. Talk, London, 2015

About the Author

Barry Oshry is a pioneer in the field of human systems thinking. His life's work has been to empower individuals and organizations by transforming system-blindness into system-sight. The educational programs he has developed include *The Power Lab*, the *Organization Workshop on Creating Partnership*, and the *When Cultures Meet Workshop*. In 2013 he launched *The Worldwide Week of Partnership*, during which Power+Systems trainers across the globe conduct pro bono partnership events for educational, charitable, advocacy, and service organizations in their local communities. In 2015 he received a Lifetime Achievement Award from the International Organization Development Network.

Barry is the author of *The Systems Letter, Seeing Systems, Leading Systems, In the Middle,* and *The Possibilities of Organization*. He is also a playwright whose stage productions include "What a Way to Make a Living," "Hierarchy," "Power Play," and "Peace." In 1975 he and his wife and partner, Karen Ellis Oshry, founded Power+Systems, Inc. whose worldwide network of trainers continues the work of empowering individuals and organizations by transforming system-blindness into system-sight.

barry@powerandsystems.com

www.powerandsystems.com
www.worldwideweekofpartnership.org

About the Publisher

Triarchy Press is a small independent publisher of new and alternative thinking about government, finance, organizations, society, movement, performance, walking and the creative life. Other Triarchy authors whose books seek to raise awareness of the importance of systems in organizational and daily life include:

Russell Ackoff	*Management f-Laws: How Organizations Really Work* *Differences that Make a Difference* *Systems Thinking for Curious Managers* *The Cake*
Rosalind Armson	*Growing Wings on the Way: Systems Thinking for Messy Situations*
Nora Bateson	*Small Arcs of Larger Circles*
Margaret Hannah	*Humanising Healthcare*
Graham Leicester	*Transformative Innovation: A guide to practice and policy*
John Seddon	*Systems Thinking in the Public Sector* *The Whitehall Effect*
Bill Sharpe	*Three Horizons: The patterning of hope*
William Tate	*The Search for Leadership* *Systemic Leadership Toolkit*
Daniel Wahl	*Designing Regenerative Cultures*

For details of all these authors and titles, please visit:

www.triarchypress.net

Printed in the USA
CPSIA information can be obtained
at www.ICGtesting.com
LVHW052122290224
773010LV00006B/12